101 Atlanta
Sports Legends

Cover and interior design by Kim Sammartano
Cover photography by Lance Davies

Copyright 2009 by Tim Darnell

TABLE OF CONTENTS

Atlanta Sports Legends
(in alphabetical order)

Aaron, Hank 2
Andersen, Morten 4
Anderson, Kenny 6
Andrews, William 7
Appling, Luke 8
Barnes, Tommy 10
Barron, Gayle 12
Bartkowski, Steve 13
Bennett, Leeman 15
Bisher, Furman 17
Blank, Arthur 18
Brogdon, Cindy 20
Brown, Kevin 21
Carey, Skip, & Van Wieren, Pete .23
Castleberry, Clint 24
Ciraldo, Al 25
Cohen, Natalie 26
Cousins, Tom 27
Cox, Bobby 29
Craig, Jim 32
Creel, Wayman 34
Cremins, Bobby 35
Curry, Bill 36
Dodd, Bobby 38
Doyal, R.L. "Shorty" 40
Driesell, Lefty 41
Duval, David 43
Duvall, Edith McGuire 45
Elliott, Bill 46
Fowlkes, Douglas Linton "Buddy" 48
Fraser, Alexa 49
Frazier, Walt 50
Garciaparra, Nomar 52
Garlington, Frances Poole King ..53
Geoffrion, Bernie "Boom Boom" .54
Glavine, Tom; Maddux, Greg; and Smoltz, John 56
Grady, Henry W. 60
Grant, Bryan Bitsy 61
Hamm, Edward 62
Hammonds, Tom 63
Haney, Lee 64
Hansford, Anne Paradise 65
Harden, Rev. John and Billie 66
Harpering, Matt 68
Harvey, B.T. 69
Harwell, Ernie 70
Heisman, John 71
Holyfield, Evander 73
Hudson, Lou 75
Humphrey, Claude 77
Hyder, John Whack 79
Johnson, Ernie 80
Jones, Bobby 81
Jones, Calvin "Monk" 83
Jones, Rosie 84
Kaiser, Roger 86
King, Kim 87
Lundquist, Steve 89
Maloof, George 90
Mann, Earl 92
Maravich, Pete 94
McFerrin, T. 96
McKay, Antonio 97
Mize, Larry 98
Moon, Johnny 99
Moses, Edwin 100
Murphy, Dale 101
Nelson, Larry 102
Neikro, Phil 103
1938 Atlanta Black Crackers ...105
1995 Atlanta Braves 107

Nobis, Tommy 108
Outlar, Jesse 110
Payne, Billy 111
Peeples, Nat 113
Pinholster, Garland 115
Powell, Charles Abner 116
Price, Mark 117
Reeves, Dan 118
Rhino, Randy 120
Rice, Homer 121
Richards, Paul 123
Rodgers, Pepper 125
Ross, Bobby 126
Salley, John 128
Sandow, Pearl 129
Schuerholz, John 130
Simpson, Tim 132
Singleton, Mildred McDaniel ..133
Smith, Rankin 134
Smith, Robert William "Red" ..136
Suggs, Louise 137
Torrence, Gwen 139
Tuggle, Jesse 140
Turner, Ted 141
Van Note, Jeff 143
Varitek, Jason 144
Wilkens, Lenny 145
Wilkins, Dominique 146
Wyatt, John Whitlow 148
Yunkus, Rich 149

ALSO:
Atlanta's Historic Sporting Venues ..150
The Atlanta Sports Hall of Fame ..154
The Atlanta Sports Council 156

101 ATLANTA
SPORTS LEGENDS

101 Atlanta's Sports Legends By Category

AUTO RACING
Bill Elliott 46

BASEBALL
1938 Atlanta Black Crackers ... 105
1995 Atlanta Braves 107
Hank Aaron 2
Luke Appling 8
Kevin Brown 21
Bobby Cox 29
Nomar Garciaparra 52
Rev. John and Billie Harden 66
Dale Murphy 101
Phil Neikro 103
Nat Peeples 113
Paul Richards 123
Pearl Sandow 129
Tom Glavine, Greg Maddux &
John Smoltz 56
Jason Varitek 144
John Whitlow Wyatt 148

BASKETBALL
Kenny Anderson 6
Cindy Brogdon 20
Pete Maravich 94
Bobby Cremins 35
Lefty Driesell 41
Walt Frazier 50
Tom Hammonds 63
Anne Paradise Hansford 65
Matt Harpring 68
Lou Hudson 75
John Whack Hyder 79
Roger Kaiser 86
Mark Price 117
John Salley 128
Lenny Wilkens 145
Dominique Wilkins 146
Rich Yunkus 149

BODYBUILDING
Lee Haney 64

BOXING/MARTIAL ARTS
Evander Holyfield 73

COACHES
Wayman Creel 34
R.L. "Shorty" Doyal 40
B.T. Harvey 69
T. McFerrin 96
Calvin "Monk" Jones 83
Johnny Moon 99
George Maloof 90
Garland Pinholster 115

EXECUTIVES
Arthur Blank 18
Tom Cousins 27
Earl Mann 92
Billy Payne 111
Charles Abner Powell 116
Homer Rice 121
John Schuerholz 130
Rankin Smith 134
Ted Turner 141

FOOTBALL
Morten Andersen 4
William Andrews 7
Steve Bartkowski 13
Leeman Bennett 15
Clint Castleberry 24
Bill Curry 36
Bobby Dodd 38
John Heisman 71
Claude Humphrey 77
Kim King 87
Tommy Nobis 108
Dan Reeves 118
Randy Rhino 120
Pepper Rodgers 125
Bobby Ross 126
Jesse Tuggle 140
Jeff Van Note 143

GOLF
Tommy Barnes 10
David Duval 43
Alexa Fraser 49
Bobby Jones 81
Rosie Jones 84
Larry Mize 98
Larry Nelson 102
Tim Simpson 132
Louise Suggs 137

HOCKEY
Jim Craig 32
Bernie "Boom Boom" Geoffrion . . .54

JOURNALISTS
Furman Bisher 17
Skip Carey & Pete Van Wieren
Al Ciraldo 25
Henry W. Grady 60
Ernie Harwell 70
Ernie Johnson 80
Jesse Outlar 110

SWIMMING
Steve Lundquist 89

TENNIS
Natalie Cohen 26
Bryan Bitsy Grant 61

TRACK & FIELD
Gayle Barron 12
Douglas Linton "Buddy" Fowlkes . . .48
Edith McGuire Duvall 45
Edward Hamm 62
Antonio McKay 97
Edwin Moses 100
Mildred McDaniel Singleton . . .133
Robert William "Red" Smith . . .136
Gwen Torrance 139

TRAPSHOOTING
Frances Poole King Garlington . . .53

AUTHOR'S FOREWORD

Believe it or not, at a time when our sports pages are dominated by the exploits of Ryan and Chipper; when our coliseums and stadiums are among the world's biggest and finest; and when our metropolis has more than its allotment of professional sports franchises; it's easy to forget that Atlanta has only been a major league sports city for about 40 years.

Nonetheless, Atlanta was a sports capital long before the Braves and Falcons came to town in the late '60s, and produced athletes and executives - whose prowess both on the field and off – laid the foundation for the city's current reputation as a sports Mecca.

As you might imagine, the hardest part of writing a book like this is determining who should be considered as an Atlanta Sports Legend, and who shouldn't. There are many of my own personal favorites and heroes who did not make the final cut.

And, as a journalist, I know there are fewer undertakings fraught with more peril than compiling a list. For virtually every publication of which I've been associated, any edition that ranked, numbered, bulleted or otherwise listed any group of individuals was inevitably the most popular undertaking of the year – as well as being the most perilous, and the most controversial. There are few professions more subjective that writing, and there is absolutely no more subjective undertaking than creating a list.

So who exactly deserves to be called an Atlanta Sports Legend? In this book, you'll find individuals who were born in Atlanta and made their athletic reputation here, but also elsewhere; you'll find athletes who hail from other parts of the nation, but who perhaps attended local Atlanta high schools and/or colleges, where their athletic prowess and complete dedication to their craft first began to be noticed, and perhaps might still remain in those respective record books. And here also are individuals who put down roots in my hometown while their career was in full bloom, and may still be here today.

And there are more than 101 biographies contained in these pages. In many of the entries, I've mentioned other notable individuals whose athletic accomplishments might not be as lengthy or impactful as the Legends' themselves, but are nonetheless worthy of praise and recognition. Many members of the Georgia Sports Hall of Fame – with even the most remote of Atlanta connections – can be found here, in some varying degree or another.

You'll also find some short pieces on a few friends of mine: the Atlanta Sports Hall of Fame and the Atlanta Sports Council, and the roles that these organizations play in ensuring Atlanta remains a national – if not global – location for major sporting events. I've been involved with both of them for many, many years, so I beg your forgiveness if I neglect any pretext of impartiality.

After reading these stories, you may come to the conclusion that some deserve to be called Legends, while others don't. That's fine with me. And if such an opinion might prompt a reader to undertake a research and literary project of their own … well, a writer can receive no greater reward than motivating someone else to join the debate.

101 ATLANTA
SPORTS LEGENDS

DEDICATION

To T.C., who has already mastered 'Smoltzie's windup, 'Bart's drop-back, and Milo Hamilton's delivery.

101 Atlanta
Sports Legends

HENRY AARON

The mighty shoulders that once propelled baseballs into the furthest reaches of the atmosphere later bore the heavy mantle of a large business empire, but during the course of his athletic career, Aaron bore a much heavier burden as he closed in on the game's most sacred milestone.

Approaching the record of 714 home runs that George Herman "Babe" Ruth had smashed out of ballparks from New England to the Midwest, Aaron – arguably one of the most talented yet unassuming men to ever play the game – endured years of media scrutiny, racism and death threats.

Born Feb. 5, 1934, in a part of Mobile, AL, called Down The Bay - a poor area of town populated mostly by blacks - Aaron's family moved to a better area of Mobile called Toulminville, where he was raised. In high school, Aaron played shortstop and third base and was an outstanding hitter, though he batted cross-handed.

In 1952, Aaron quit high school and joined the Indianapolis Clowns of the Negro American League. After a brief stay as their shortstop, his contract was sold in June for $10,000 to the Braves, who beat out the New York Giants for his services. That summer, he was the Northern League's Rookie of the Year for Eau Claire, Wis., despite playing only 87 games. In 1953, Aaron became one of the South Atlantic League's first five black players. He moved from shortstop to second base, and though faced with the racism of the South, he sparked Jacksonville to the Sally League pennant by leading the league in batting (.362), RBIs (125), runs (115) and hits (208), and was voted the league's MVP.

At spring training the next year, it didn't look like the 20-year-old Aaron would make the Braves. But when Bobby Thomson suffered a broken ankle sliding into second, the Braves needed an outfielder to replace him, and the 6-foot, 160-pound Aaron won the competition, taking over as the regular left fielder. In 1957, he hit a home run to help the Braves clinch the division (a moment that Aaron would later describe as his career's greatest moment), and later helped lead the team to a World Series championship.

Over the course of his 23-year major league career, Aaron hit 20 or more homers for 20 consecutive years; at least 30 in 15 seasons; and 40 or better eight times. His lifetime numbers are stratospheric – .305 batting average; 3,298 games; 12,364 at-bats; 3,771 hits; 2,174 runs scored; and 2,297 RBIs. He also was the first big leaguer to total 3,000 hits and 500 home runs. He was voted into the Baseball Hall of Fame with the highest vote total at that time, 406.

Once thought to be untouchable, Ruth's record of 714 was tied by Aaron at the beginning of the '74 season, setting the stage for the fateful evening contest of April 8, against the Los Angeles Dodgers. The Braves were opening their home season that evening at Atlanta Stadium and all of the sporting world was focused on the city for that one swing that would propel Aaron into immortality.

In the fourth inning, after walking Aaron in the second, Dodger pitcher Al Downing's first pitch to Aaron was down in the dirt. Next, Downing delivered a high fastball, and with a whip of the bat - his first swing of the evening, at 9:07 pm - Aaron sent the specially marked ball into the Braves bullpen in left-center, approximately 400 feet from home plate. Left fielder Bill Buckner jumped high in an attempt to intercept history, but he had no chance to reach it.

The large message board in left-center flashed "715," and just like that, Aaron was the all-time home run king. The crowd roared for a full 10 minutes as Aaron was mobbed by teammates, relatives, friends and well-wishers. Aaron said after the game, "The home run wouldn't have really meant that much to me if we hadn't won the game. Five years ago, I never thought I'd be in this position, but now that I am, I'm sure glad it's over with."

Aaron would hit 18 more home runs that year for the Braves, and then finish his career in the town in which his major league career had started, Milwaukee, hitting 12 in 1975 and 10 in 1976, for 755 total major league home runs.

Aaron was part of the inaugural Atlanta Sports Hall of Fame class.

What They've Said: *"Is this to be the year in which Aaron, at the age of 39, takes a moon walk above one of the most hallowed individual records in American sport...? Or will it be remembered as the season in which Aaron, the most dignified of athletes, was besieged with hate mail and trapped by the cobwebs and goblins that lurk in baseball's attic?"*

— Sports Illustrated

BY THE NUMBERS

CAREER STATISTICS
Aaron business empire and as HOF ref.

G	AB	R	H	HR	RBI	BB	SO	Avg.	SLG
3,298	12,364	2,174	3,771	755	2,297	1,402	1,383	.305	.555

LET'S DON'T FORGET:

Milo Hamilton. The 1992 recipient of the Ford C. Frick Award ... Called some 9,000 games and broadcast major league baseball for more than 40 years, including from 1966-75 with the Atlanta Braves ... Was behind the microphone for the Atlanta Braves during arguably the biggest moment in American baseball history when he called Aaron's 715th home run: "There's a drive to left-center field! That ball is gonna be ... outta here! It's gone! It's 715! There's a new home run champion of all time! And it's Henry Aaron! Henry Aaron's coming around third! His teammates are at home plate! And listen to this crowd!"

MORTEN ANDERSEN

The all-time leading scorer in NFL history, Andersen retired in late 2008, after playing his final NFL season for the Atlanta Falcons in 2007, a season in which the native of Denmark was the league's oldest active player.

As a student, Andersen was a gymnast and a long jumper, and barely missed becoming a member of the Danish junior national soccer team. He visited the United States in 1977 as a Youth For Understanding exchange student. He first kicked an American football on a whim at Ben Davis High School in Indianapolis. He was so impressive in his one season of high school football that he was given a scholarship to Michigan State University.

Andersen starred at Michigan State, setting several records, including a Big Ten Conference record 63-yard field goal against Ohio State University. He was named an All American in 1981. His success landed him the kicking job with the New Orleans Saints.

Andersen's NFL career got off to a rocky start. On his first NFL kickoff to start the 1982 season, Andersen twisted his ankle and missed eight weeks of the season. Despite the early setback, he soon emerged as one of the NFL's strongest and most reliable placekickers. In his years with the Saints, he was named to six Pro Bowls, kicked 302 field goals, and scored 1318 points. In 1991, against Chicago, Andersen kicked a 60-yard field goal, tying him with Steve Cox for the second-longest field goal in league history at the time. Andersen's proficiency with field goal kicking earned him the nickname "Mr. Automatic." Following the 1994 season, he was released by the Saints for salary cap purposes and because his accuracy had started to decline.

Andersen signed with the Atlanta Falcons, and in December 1995 against the Saints, he became the first player in NFL history to kick three field goals of over 50 yards in a single game.

In 1998, he kicked a game-winning field goal in overtime in the NFC championship game to beat the Minnesota Vikings and send the Falcons to its first-ever Super Bowl appearance.

Andersen went on to play with the New York Giants for the 2001 season, followed by the Kansas City Chiefs the following two seasons. Before 2004 season, Andersen was released by the Chiefs, and he signed by the Vikings. Having not been signed by a team following the 2004 season, he became a free agent and did not play in 2005.

In January 2006, Andersen was inducted as the first member of the Danish American Football Federation Hall of Fame. Later that year, Andersen returned to the NFL, re-signing with the Falcons. In his second game back, Andersen made five of five field goals, matching his career best for the ninth time, as well as both extra point attempts. He was named NFC special teams player of the week, becoming the oldest player to earn the honor since the award was first introduced in 1984. He is also the team record holder for both the New Orleans Saints and the Atlanta Falcons for overall points scored.

On Dec. 16, 2006, Andersen passed Gary Anderson to become the all-time leading scorer in NFL history. The following weekend, Andersen again passed Anderson to become the NFL's career leader in field goals made. On Sept. 17, 2007, Andersen re-signed with the Falcons in an attempt to secure their unreliable kicking game. In fact, by the end of what turned out to be his final season, Andersen was 25-for-28 on field goals (89.3 percent), the most accurate season of his career.

BY THE NUMBERS

As of the end of the 2008 NFL season, Andersen held these NFL records:

Most games played (career) - 382
Most field goals attempted (career) - 709
Most field goals (career) - 565
Most points (career) - 2,544
Most seasons, 79 or more points - 24
Most seasons, 90 or more points - 22
Most seasons, 98 or more points - 18
Most seasons, 99 or more points - 16
Most field goals attempted of 50 or more yards (total) - 84
Most field goals (50 or more yards) (total) - 40 (tied with Jason Hanson)
Most field goals (50 or more yards) in a season - 8
Most field goals (50 or more yards) in a game - 3 (vs. New Orleans, Dec. 10, 1995) (tied with Neil Rackers and Kris Brown)
Most consecutive games with a point (career) - 346
Most points in Pro Bowl (total) - 45 (15 points after touchdown, 10 field goals)
Most points after touchdown in Pro Bowl (total) - 15
Most field goal attempts in Pro Bowl (total) - 18
Most field goals in Pro Bowl (total) - 10

Andersen currently holds 2nd place in the following NFL records:

Most points after touchdown attempted (career) - 859
Most points after touchdown made (career) - 849
Most seasons - 25
Most seasons, 100 or more points - 14

LET'S DON'T FORGET:

Chris Chandler. Quarterback for the Atlanta Falcons from 1997-2001 ... Helped lead the Falcons to their best record in history in 1998 (14-2) and to the franchise's only Super Bowl (1998).

KENNY ANDERSON

One of the greatest players in Georgia Tech basketball history, Anderson enjoyed an All-Star career in the National Basketball Association.

Anderson, who became a 13-year NBA veteran, was the Atlantic Coast Conference Rookie of the Year and National Freshman of the Year in 1989-90, when he helped the Jackets to the NCAA Final Four. The following year he was a consensus first-team all-American and NBA lottery pick.

Anderson was selected after his sophomore season by the New Jersey Nets in the first round of the 1991 draft, where he became the all-time leader in Nets' franchise history with 2,363 assists and 6th with 476 steals and 8th with 4,655 points. He also made the 1994 NBA All-Star Game as a starter, scoring six points in 16 minutes.

One of the league's strongest point guards, Anderson had a long and well-traveled career in the NBA. He was traded to the Charlotte Hornets in 1996, and signed as a free agent with the Portland Trail Blazers later that year. In 1978, he was shipped to the Toronto Raptors, and later was traded to the Boston Celtics, where he started 76 games and helped the Celtics reach the Eastern Conference Finals.

In 2002, Anderson was traded to the Seattle SuperSonics, and later made the New Orleans Hornets squad that year. He signed with the Indiana Pacers as a free agent in 2003, and returned to the home of his alma mater in 2004, when the Atlanta Hawks signed him, again as a free agent. He finished out that season as a Los Angeles Clipper.

Anderson was always at the top of his team and the league in scoring, steals and assists. He swiped the 1,000th steal of his career against the San Antonio Spurs on Feb. 23, 2001, and logged more than 400 assists for the seventh time in his career in 2001-02. Anderson scored his 10,000th career point against the Miami Heat on Dec. 7, 2002.

LET'S DON'T FORGET:

Pete Silas. 1953 All-SEC selection for Georgia Tech ... Named to the 1952 SEC All-Tournament team ... Third-team All-SEC in 1951 ... Finished career with 1,084 points (15.1 per game) ... Three-year starter at the forward position ... Drafted by the Minneapolis Lakers ... Member of the 1955 U.S. basketball team that won gold at the Pan-American Games ... Member of the Georgia Tech Hall of Fame.

WILLIAM ANDREWS

The NFL's most productive running back for five consecutive years was originally a third-round, 79th draft pick out of Auburn University. Yet when Andrews made his professional debut in 1979, he set a then-Falcons record, rushing for 167 yards on 30 carries against the New Orleans Saints, on his way to becoming only the 12th rookie in NFL history to gain more than 1,000 yards rushing (1,023).

Born in Thomasville, Ga., Andrews was one of the greatest players in Atlanta Falcons" history. No. 31, his neck encased by a white, horseshoe-shaped support collar, plowed through defenders for 5,986 yards on 1,315 carries from 1979-83. He played in four consecutive Pro Bowls, and averaged 4.55 yards per carry. Rushing for 100 or more yards 22 times, Andrews caught 276 passes for 2,645 yards, and still holds the club record with 8,702 combined yards and four 1,000-yard seasons.

Andrews became just the second running back in NFL history to have two 2,000-yard all-purpose seasons (the first was O.J. Simpson.) When he had his first 2,000-yard year, he joined just four other backs (Jim Brown, Walter Payton, Wilbert Montgomery and Simpson).

Andrews led all NFL running backs from 1979-83 in 8,382 yards rushing and receiving. He tallied 246 points during his Falcon career, scoring 41 career touchdowns (30 rushing). Andrews made 63 consecutive starts during his career, and 72 of 73 games before disaster struck.

In August 1984, Andrews tore the ligaments, cartilage and nerves in his knee during training camp. Two years later, and after 660 days of rehabilitation, Andrews returned to play one more season. In 2004, the Falcons inducted him into their inaugural Ring of Honor.

LET'S DON'T FORGET:

Doug Wycoff. Second team All American at Georgia Tech in 1924 and 1925 ... Member of the Georgia Tech Hall of Fame ... Enjoyed a six year career in the NFL with the New York Giants (1927 and 1931); Staten Island (1929-1930, 1932); and Boston (1934) ... Threw for eight career TDs and rushed for 11.

Eddie Lee Ivery. Graduated from an east Georgia high school as the nation's most sought-after running back ... Signed with Georgia Tech ... Set an NCAA single-game rushing record of 356 yards and a single-season rushing record of 1,562 yards ... Rushed for 3,517 yards, third highest in Tech history ... 4,325 all-purpose yards, also third best in Jacket history ... Broke seven Tech rushing records and was selected to the Associated Press and United Press International All-American Football teams ... In 1978 Tech visited Air Force. In a blinding storm, with a wind-chill factor of zero and three inches of snow, Ivery set his NCAA single-game record with touchdown runs of 80, 73 and 57 yards ... No. 1 draft pick in 1979 by the Green Bay Packers ... Played six seasons with the Packers.

LUKE APPLING

One of only two former Atlanta Crackers in the National Baseball Hall of Fame, Appling spent 20 seasons with the Chicago White Sox, years that were so productive that in a 1969 fan poll, he was tagged the greatest living White Sox player.

Born in High Point, N.C., Appling was an All-City baseball player at Fulton High School. He participated in three sports at Atlanta's Oglethorpe University. In football, he was a halfback on the Oglethorpe squad that upset the University of Georgia in 1929, and on the diamond, he hit four home runs against Mercer in one game.

Appling's professional baseball career began in 1930 with the Southern Association's Atlanta Crackers. Appling played in 104 games with the Crackers, batting .326. He was sold to the Chicago Cubs late that year, but joined the White Sox through a cash transaction that involved another Cracker, outfielder Doug Taitt.

There was nothing remarkable about Appling's first two seasons. But the arrival of Jimmy Dykes as manager in 1934 had a positive effect on the young shortstop. Dykes cajoled, pleaded, and instilled confidence. When Appling finally realized that he wasn't going to drive the ball out of Comiskey Park, he adjusted his stance and became one of the most productive hitters of the decade. He would foul off pitch after pitch before selecting just the right one, or drawing one of his many bases on balls. Legend has it that on one occasion, Appling fouled off 17 straight pitches before hitting a triple, and his 1,302 lifetime walks (with a high of 122 in 1935) ranks 25th all-time.

In 1936, Appling led the American League with a .388 average. It was the first batting title won by a White Sox player. He also had a club-record 27-game hitting streak and a seven-for-seven performance over three games. In 1943, at age 35, he won his second batting title. He hit .300 15 times.

Over his career, Appling played in 2,422 games but never made the post-season. He played 2,218 games at shortstop, and in 8,857 at bats, he recorded 2,749 hits, 440 of which were doubles along with 102 triples. He also scored 1,319 runs and drove in 1,116. Only three times during his career did he bat below .300.

Appling held down the shortstop position for nearly 20 years. In spite of his everyday play, he acquired the epithet "Old Aches & Pains" through 20 years of complaining about his various physical ailments, the condition of the infield, and salary disputes, among other things.

Elected to the Hall of Fame in 1964, Appling worked as a batting instructor for the Atlanta Braves in the 1980s. He died in 1991, at the age of 83, in Cumming, GA.

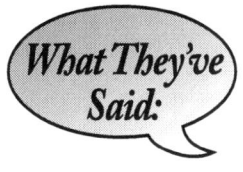

"Few were better or more deadly with two strikes than Appling. He just waited for the pitch he wanted and lashed into it."

— Arthur Daley, sportswriter

BY THE NUMBERS

CAREER STATISTICS

Batting average: .310
Hits: 2,749
Runs batted in: 1,116

TEAMS

As player –
Chicago White Sox (1930-1950)

As manager –
Kansas City Athletics (1967)

CAREER HIGHLIGHTS AND AWARDS

- 7x All-Star selection (1936, 1939, 1940, 1941, 1943, 1946, 1947)
- Led AL in batting average in 1936 and 1943
- Chicago White Sox #4 retired

LET'S DON'T FORGET:

James Tolbert Hearn. Born in Atlanta ... Posted a 109-89 record during a 13-year major league career with the St. Louis Cardinals (1947-1950), New York Giants (1950-1956) and Philadelphia Phillies (1957-1959) ... Career winning percentage of .551 with a 3.81 ERA, 396 games and 229 complete games ... Went 1-0 for the Giants in the 1947 World Series against the New York Yankees ... Led the league in ERA in 1950 with a 2.49 mark ... Won 12 or more games four times ... Best season came in 1951 with a 17-9 record.

TOMMY BARNES

A close friend of Bobby Jones, Barnes would break most of the legendary golfer's records during a career that would span into his 70s.

A native of Monroe, GA, Barnes qualified for the National Amateur tournament 16 consecutive times. He won the 1935 and 1937 Atlantic City Amateur, and in 1938, led Georgia Tech to the Southern Intercollegiate title, serving as team captain in '37 and '38.

Barnes captured the 1941 Georgia amateur crown, and won the Bobby Jones Four Ball Meet and the Dogwood Tournament five times each. The 1946 Southeastern PGA Open and the Southeastern Amateur were his, as were the 1947 and 1949 Southern Amateur.

Barnes became involved with the Southern Golf Association (SGA) in 1940 at the Southern Amateur, where at the time he was the SGA's Southern States Four-Ball Champion. He would go on to repeat as the Southern States Four-Ball Champion in 1941, 1946 and 1947.

Barnes played the last round of golf with Jones before the Atlanta Sports Legend was sidelined with a neurological disorder. Barnes is given chief credit for preserving Jones' home course, the East Lake Country Club, when he orchestrated a move among Jones' friends to buy the facility from the Atlanta Athletic Club in 1967 when the club was relocating to Duluth. At age 73, Barnes shot a 62 at East Lake Country Club, which broke Jones' record of 63 set in 1922.

The Georgia State Golf Association's Tommy Barnes Award signifies the GSGA's overall player of the year. It was established in 1998. The Tommy Barnes Award winner is selected each year by the GSGA's Championship Committee.

Barnes is a member of the Georgia Tech, Southern Golf, Atlanta Athletic Club, Georgia Golf and Georgia Sports halls of fame. And, in 2007, Barnes was inducted into the Atlanta Sports Hall of Fame.

BY THE NUMBERS

1934	Southern Interscholastic Champion
1938	Southern Intercollegiate Champion
1939	Low Sectional Qualifier in US for U. S. Amateur
1940	Southern States Four-Ball Champion
1941	Southern States Four-Ball Champion
1941	Georgia State Amateur Champion
1946	Southern States Four-Ball Champion
1946	Southeastern PGA Open Champion
1946	Southeastern Open Champion
1947	Southern States Four-Ball Champion
1950	1st Alternate to Walker Cup Team

LET'S DON'T FORGET:

Charlie Yates. Owner of what *Life Magazine* called "the best grin in golf" ... An Atlanta native who won the 1938 British Amateur ... Captured the 1943 NCAA individual golf title in 1934 and the 1935 Western Amateur ... 1931 and 1932 Georgia State Amateur Golf champion ... Five times the low scoring amateur at The Masters ... Captained the 1953 U.S. Walker Cup team and played on the 1936 and '38 teams ... Played with Bobby Jones in his final round in 1948 at East Lake Golf Club ... National college champion while at Georgia Tech (1934).

Danny Yates, III. An Atlanta native who was three-time Georgia State Amateur champion (1977, '89, and '96) ... 1974 Southern Amateur champion ... Three-time winner of the Georgia-Mid Amateur (1983, '85, '94) ... 1992 U.S. Mid-Amateur champion ... 1988 U.S. Amateur runner-up ... Member of the 1988 W.S. World Amateur team ... Played in the 1989 and '93 Masters' Tournaments as an amateur ... Made the cut in the 1971 U.S. Open.

GAYLE BARRON

An Atlanta native, Barron is truly one of the pioneers of American road racing. The winner of the first Peachtree Road Race in 1970, Barron went on to win five of the first six, earning her the title of "the First Lady of Peachtree," and remains the winningest athlete in Peachtree Road Race history. Barron won the 1978 Boston Marathon (Women's Division) in a personal record time of 2:44.52, the second-fastest Boston Marathon run by a female up to that point.

She also won three Atlanta Peach Bowl Marathons; over her career she ran a total of 26 marathons as well as numerous other races, and her best 10K time was 35:20.

From 1976-78, Barron was ranked among the top female marathoners in the world. The United States' second-best female marathoner in 1978, Barron ranked as the third-best in 1976 and 1977. The first woman to run a marathon in the South, Barron competed in 23 marathons and never placed lower than fifth.

Barron was a world-class runner who literally traveled the world. She finished fifth in the 1975 New York City Marathon (2:57:22); third in the 1976 Honolulu Marathon (2:52:16); and third overall (second among U.S. runners) at the 1976 Women's International Marathon in Waldneil, West Germany. She garnered third place in the 1977 New York City Marathon (2:52:19); and fourth at the 1978 Women's International Marathon held in Atlanta.

But Barron transcended her sport in a way that few others had at that time. She has been named by the United States Jaycees as one of American's Top 10 Healthy American Fitness Leaders, and *Runner's World Magazine* once referred to Barron as the "First Lady" of running. She also authored a book, "The Beauty of Running."

With a journalism degree from the University of Georgia, Barron was sought after as a running commentator and also appeared on ABC's "Good Morning America" and on other major television stations across the country. Recognized as an expert resource on running and fitness, Barron was featured in *Self, Runner's World Magazine, Ms, Glamour, Vie, Sport and Fitness* and *USA Today*, among other periodicals.

In 2007, Barron was inducted into the Atlanta Sports Hall of Fame.

STEVE BARTKOWSKI

The Falcons' No. 1 draft choice in 1975, Bartkowski broke into the lineup as a rookie and was named the NFL's Rookie of the Year after throwing for 1,662 yards and 15 touchdowns. Over the next 11 seasons, the quarterback out of the University of California was an All-Pro twice and offensive MVP of the NFC following a magical 1980 season, and was the NFL's leading passer three times during his prolific career.

"Bart" led the Falcons to their first divisional championships in 1980 and 1982 and Falcon records for most touchdown passes in a season (31); most passing yards in a season (3,830); most career passing yards (23,468); and most career touchdown passes (154). He led the NFL in quarterback rating in 1983 (97.6) and completion percentage in 1984.

Bartkowski overcame numerous knee injuries to set every club record in passing that included 23,468 yards and 154 touchdown passes in his 123 Falcons games. He led the Falcons to their first-ever playoff berth in 1978 and division title in 1980. A third playoff berth followed in 1982. His 1983 interception ratio of 1.16 (five in 432 attempts) was second-lowest in NFL history. Bartkowski once threw 197 straight passes without an interception, a club record.

Producing three seasons of 3,000 yards or more passing, Bartkowski also had 12 games of more than 300 yards passing, and two seasons of 30 or more touchdown passes. A clutch performer, he once started 56 consecutive games and had a game-winning or game-tying touchdown pass five times in the Falcons' first playoff of 1978. A pair of fourth quarter touchdowns led the Falcons to their first playoff win over the Philadelphia Eagles on Dec. 24, 1978.

Bartkowski was one of the original inductees into the Atlanta Falcons' Ring of Honor, and in 2008, he was inducted into the Atlanta Sports Hall of Fame.

(Continued on next page)

STEVE BARTKOWSKI

BY THE NUMBERS

Year	TM	G	Comp	Att	PCT	YD	Y/A	TD	INT
1975	ATL	11	115	255	45.1	1662	6.5	13	15
1976	ATL	5	57	120	47.5	677	5.6	2	9
1977	ATL	8	64	136	47.1	796	5.9	5	13
1978	ATL	14	187	369	50.7	2489	6.7	10	18
1979	ATL	14	204	380	53.7	2505	6.6	17	20
1980	ATL	16	257	463	55.5	3544	7.7	31	16
1981	ATL	16	297	533	55.7	3829	7.2	30	23
1982	ATL	9	166	262	63.4	1905	7.3	8	11
1983	ATL	14	274	432	63.4	3167	7.3	22	5
1984	ATL	11	181	269	67.3	2158	8.0	11	10
1985	ATL	5	69	111	62.2	738	6.6	5	1
1986	LA	6	61	126	48.4	654	5.2	2	3
TOTAL		129	1932	3456	55.9	24124	7.0	156	144

LET'S DON'T FORGET:

Maxie Baughan. Member of the Philadelphia Eagles' 1960 world championship team, the last time the franchise won the equivalent of the title ... Enjoyed a 12-year NFL career with the Eagles (1960-65), Los Angeles Rams (1966-70) and Washington Redskins (1971) ... Captained Tech's 1956 freshman team, and was a Consensus All-American center in 1959 ... Also named SEC Lineman of the Year in '59 by the Atlanta Touchdown Club ... Tech's Athlete of the Year for 1959-60 ... Captained the team's Gator Bowl squad where he was named Defensive Player of the Game ... Also played in the 1960 Hula Bowl.

Chip Kell. An Atlanta native and two-sport star (track & field and football) in high school and college ... 1965, 1966 and 1967 Atlanta Track Club "Track Man of the Year" ... 1966 *Scholastic Magazine's* All-America Track and Field Team ... 1969 and 1970 All-American lineman at the University of Tennessee ...Drafted in the 17th round of the 1971 NFL Draft by the San Diego Chargers ... Played in Canadian Football League with the Edmonton Eskimos in 1971 and 1972 ... Won numerous trophies in shot put and set numerous records throughout the south and the nation ... Consensus All-American lineman (*Playboy Magazine*, *Look Magazine*, UPI, AP, Football Writers', Walter Camp, Kodak, Newspaper Enterprise Association) in 1970 ... All-SEC ... Finalist for the Lombardi Award as the nation's top lineman.

LEEMAN BENNETT

The winningest coach in Atlanta Falcons history began his tenure by overseeing a defense that today still holds a prominent place in NFL record books.

An assistant with the Los Angeles Rams, Bennett took over the Falcons in 1977, the final year of the league's 14-game regular season. Nicknamed the "Gritz Blitz," the defense allowed just 129 points, a record that still stands, as the league moved to a 16-game format the following year. Bennett was NFC coach of the year in 1977 as well.

Bennett coached the Falcons for five more seasons, through 1982. His teams were 46-41 in the regular season and made the playoffs three times, the team's first playoff experience coming in 1978 as a wild card, with fellow Atlanta Sports Legend Steve Bartkowski as quarterback. That was also the first time in which the Falcons won a playoff game, a 14-13 thriller against the Philadelphia Eagles. Two years later, the Falcons won their first division title, losing in the playoffs to the Dallas Cowboys. In 1982, the Falcons finished 5-4 in a strike-shortened season, and lost to the Minnesota Vikings in the postseason.

However, Bennett was fired in the aftermath, and disastrous results for the franchise followed. The team's next winning season wouldn't come until 1991. Bennett's coaching career came to an end in 1986, after two seasons with the Tampa Bay Buccaneers.

Bennett's influence on Atlanta's sports scene extended beyond his head coaching days for the Falcons, however. He remains deeply involved in leading Atlanta's college bowl game, the Chick-fil-A Bowl (formerly known as the Peach Bowl) into the national spotlight.

 *"Every once in a while, coaching runs through my veins, even today."*

— Leeman Bennett

LEEMAN BENNETT

BY THE NUMBERS

Year	TM	Reg. Season W	L	T	Playoffs W	L
1977	ATL	7	7	0	0	0
1978	ATL	9	7	0	1	1
1979	ATL	6	10	0	0	0
1980	ATL	12	4	0	0	1
1981	ATL	7	9	0	0	0
1982	ATL	5	4	0	0	1
1985	TAM	2	14	0	0	0
1986	TAM	2	14	0	0	0
TOTALS		**50**	**69**	**0**	**1**	**3**

LET'S DON'T FORGET:

Elmer B. Morrow. Coached five sports at Druid Hills High School from 1949-61 ... Basketball teams were 191-74 with three state crowns and four regional titles ... school garnered state gymnastics in 1953 and state football championship in 1956.

Sidney Scarborough. Head football coach at Tech High in 1940, 1945-46, winning the state championship in 1946 ... Served as the first Athletic Director for Atlanta high schools and stayed in that position for 17 years.

FURMAN BISHER

Acknowledged as one of the finest sports writers and columnists in American journalistic history, Bisher's words have eloquently described sports in the Peach State for more than 50 years on the pages of the *Atlanta Journal-Constitution*.

Bisher, who often described himself as the product of limited ambition, graduated in 1938 from the University of North Carolina-Chapel Hill. At 20, he became editor of the *Lumberton Voice*. Later he worked for *The High Point Enterprise* and *The Charlotte News*, where he became sports editor in 1948.

One year later, Bisher became sports editor of *The Atlanta Constitution* and, seven years later, *The Atlanta Journal*. He was chosen Georgia Sportswriter of the Year 16 times and cited by the Associated Press for having written Georgia's best sports story of the year more than 20 times. The author of seven books, Bisher was named one of the nation's five best columnists in 1961 by *Time Magazine*. Over his career, he has written more than 600 magazine stories for *Sports Illustrated*, *The Saturday Evening Post*, and countless others.

Bisher became an editor in 1940 for the *Charlotte News*, where he worked for the rest of the decade, excepting four years of service during World War II. In 1950 he left the *Charlotte News* to become sports editor for the *Atlanta Constitution*. In 1957 he joined the Atlanta Journal and the *Sunday Journal-Constitution* as sports editor and columnist, and he continues to write for the Atlanta Journal-Constitution. He also became a columnist for the *Sporting News*.

Over the years Bisher scored a number of memorable journalistic coups. His first occurred in 1949, when "Shoeless" Joe Jackson gave Bisher and *Sport Magazine* his only interview since 1919, the year Jackson was ousted from baseball in the "Black Sox" scandal.

In 2007, he was inducted into the Atlanta Sports Hall of Fame.

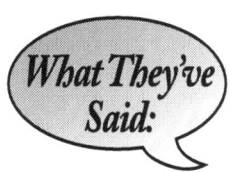

"There's no story there, really, until Bisher acknowledges it. Once he does, you know it's a story and has some substance. The man is a talent; a true talent."

— Ralph McGill, The Atlanta Constitution

ARTHUR BLANK

When Blank purchased the Atlanta Falcons in 2002, The Home Depot's co-founder brought his own successful style and managerial approach to one of the league's least successful franchises, and immediately made his presence known to fans and players alike.

Anyone who needs evidence that Blank knows how to turn around an organization's fortunes need look no further than the Falcons, a team often known more for its failures than successes. On January 4, 2003, less than a year after buying the team, Blank was on the sidelines of Lambeau Field exchanging hugs and handshakes with players and staff alike, after the Falcons became the first team in history to defeat the Green Bay Packers in a home playoff game.

After agreeing in principle to purchase the Falcons in December 2001, Blank wasted no time in applying his listening-is-what-matters-most approach. On the Falcons' charter flight back from St. Louis after the 2001 season's final game, Blank canvassed every player on the plane. His question was simple: "What can I do to help the team win?"

The answer from the players was equally simple: Fill the Georgia Dome with fans who would supply the team with the noise and energy necessary to give it a decisive home-field advantage every game. Upon the sale of the Falcons being unanimously approved by NFL owners, Blank immediately reached out and made a promise to the very constituency the players longed to see in droves every Sunday. Blank's promise to transform the Falcons began arguably the busiest off season in the NFL's history.

In almost unheard-of fashion, the Falcons lowered prices on more than 30 percent (23,000) of the Georgia Dome's seats in 2002, including offering 10,000 season tickets at $100. As a result, the Falcons sold out every home game for the first time since 1992 and welcomed more than 21,000 new season ticket holders.

To increase parking and offer more tailgating opportunities, the team secured leases on lots within blocks of the Georgia Dome. In addition, an area known as "The Gulch" was opened for thousands of fans to tailgate. In total, more than 20,000 season ticket holders were assured reserved parking with tailgating space. With the 2004 addition of parking for 10,000 more fans, the Falcons now have parking for more than 30,000 fans.

As part of enhancing the game day experience, the team introduced Falcons Landing, an outdoor entertainment area where thousands of fans enjoy interactive games, live bands and visits with former Falcons greats. In addition, the team brought in headline musical acts to perform during pregame and halftime.

The improvements have been unanimously applauded by fans. What ensued was a Georgia Dome that went from averaging 54,251 in 2001 to a venue that has sold out more than 90 percent of its preseasons and regular seasons. During the 2004 off-season, the club had a season ticket waiting list of more than 12,000 fans for the first time in its history.

Also on Blank's agenda has been acquiring players who would have an immediate impact on the team. The Falcons would become major players in the 2003 free agent market, and Blank's hands-on approach and his one-of-a-kind personal touch did not go unnoticed by players who the Falcons were courting.

In 2008, after a disastrous season the year before, Blank's Falcons made one of the NFL's most remarkable turnarounds, going 11-4 and making the playoffs. Regardless of the numerous controversies that have occurred during his tenure as owner, Blank has steadfastly held to his goal of "making Atlanta proud."

"Some owners get what the game's all about. Thank goodness for Atlanta's owner. When he took over the club he asked players what they wanted ... and they said they wanted their fans back. So Blank did what he could. Blank understands the game is not just about the players. It's about the people who pay to see them, too. Good for him. Lucky for Atlanta."

— National football writer Clark Judge, who named Blank his 2002 Executive of the Year

CINDY BROGDON

The first Georgian to be a member of the U.S. Olympic Basketball team, Brogdon was part of the 1976 silver-medal winning squad at the Montreal Summer Games.

Brogdon's prep career in Atlanta preceded her outstanding collegiate and professional career. While at Greater Atlanta Christian (GAC), she led the school to three state championships ('72, '74 and '75) and the state runner-up in 1973, earning MVP honors in the state tournament each of those years. She also set 12 GAC school records: most points in a game (44), season (802), and career (2,672); most points per game season average (27.4), and per game career average (23.7); most field goals made in a season (305) and career (237); most free throws made in a career (612); most rebounds in a season (299), and career (1,095); and best rebound career average per game (9.8).

A native of Buford, GA., Brogdon attended Mercer University as the state's first female to ever receive a full basketball scholarship. Her total of 3,204 points ranks second on the Association of Intercollegiate Athletics for Women's career scoring list. Brogdon played for the Lady Bears in 1976 and '77, during the same period in which she was an Olympian. She won the College Athlete of the Year Award while at Mercer, and set seven school records as a freshman. In 1976 she was named a Kodak All-American.

Brogdon transferred to the University of Tennessee in 1978, where she played two years for the Lady Vols and was featured in *Sports Illustrated* and *Newsweek* as one of the nation's top collegiate athletes. Her 20.1-points-per-game average led the SEC in scoring, and in 1979 she earned her second Kodak All-American honors.

Professionally, Brogdon played for the New Orleans Pride of the Women's Professional Basketball League in 1979 and '80, and ranked in the top 10 in scoring and assists while making the All-Pro squad and playing in the league's All-Star Game. She was inducted into the Women's Institute on Sport and Education Hall of Fame in 1996 and the GAC Hall of Fame in 1999, and also is recognized in the Georgia Sports Hall of Fame.

KEVIN BROWN

One of the most volatile pitchers in Major League Baseball history, Brown also was one of his era's top aces, and baseball's first $100-million man.

The Georgia Tech star made *The Sporting News'* college All-America team in 1986 with an intense, take-no-prisoners attitude that established him as one of the nation's top collegiate hurlers. Taken by the Texas Rangers in the first round of the June 1986 draft, Brown was soon in the majors, finally moving into the Rangers' starting rotation in 1989.

In his first full year with the club, Brown went 12-9 with a 3.35 ERA as the No. 2 starter behind Hall of Famer Nolan Ryan. But a spring-training adjustment the following season hurt his mechanics and led to a 9-12 record and 4.40 ERA. Brown also had the ignominious achievement of becoming only the second American League hurler in history to make 33 starts without a complete game.

After an off-season with a sports psychologist, Brown responded with his finest season in a Rangers uniform in 1992, blossoming into the staff's steadiest performer. He won 15 games the following season. Declared a free agent following the 1994 strike settlement, Brown signed a one-year contract with the Orioles, but left the club as a free agent after the season to become a cornerstone of owner Wayne Huizenga's ambitious push to put the Florida Marlins in the World Series.

Brown's first season in the National League – 1996 - brought a 17-11 record. After the season, he placed second to Atlanta's (and fellow Atlanta Sports Legend) John Smoltz in the National League Cy Young balloting. In 1997, Brown's reputation as one of the toughest pitchers ever was solidified when, suffering from a stomach virus, he threw a 142-pitch complete game in game six of the NLCS to propel the Marlins into the World Series, which they would eventually win.

Brown attracted a great deal of attention from other teams when Huizenga ordered a massive salary dump after the season. He was traded to San Diego, and Brown helped lead the Padres into their first World Series since 1984.

For the second straight year Brown entered the off-season as one of the game's most sought-after pitchers. His record-setting contract with the Dodgers - guaranteed over seven years - totaled $105 million. But after five years in LA, Brown was traded to the New York Yankees where injuries began sidelining this intensely competitive perfectionist.

(Continued on next page)

KEVIN BROWN

What They've Said: *"You go ahead and break whatever you want. As long as it's not any of my stuff and you pay for what you break, I don't care."*

— Rene Lachemann, former manager, to Brown, who had a tenacity to demolish water coolers, tables, and sometimes, anything else in his sight

BY THE NUMBERS

CAREER STATISTICS

Win-loss record 211-144

Earned run average 3.28

Strikeouts 2,397

TEAMS

- Texas Rangers (1986-1994)
- Baltimore Orioles (1995)
- Florida Marlins (1996-1997)
- San Diego Padres (1998)
- Los Angeles Dodgers (1999-2003)
- New York Yankees (2004-2005)
- Career highlights and awards
- 6x All-Star selection (1992, 1996, 1997, 1998, 2000, 2003)
- World Series champion (1997)
- 1998 NL TSN Pitcher of the Year

SKIP CARAY & PETE VAN WIEREN

For more than 30 years, the monikers "Skip and Pete" were as synonymous with the Atlanta Braves just as other Atlanta Sports Legends such as Dale Murphy, John Smoltz and John Schuerholz. The 2008 Major League Baseball season marked Caray and Van Wieren's 33rd year calling games together for the franchise.

And it was also their last, although for different reasons.

Caray began his broadcasting career at KMOX-Radio in St. Louis, MO, as host of a 15-minute high school sports show and as a high school basketball sportscaster. He later joined his father, the legendary Harry Caray, as a color commentator for University of Missouri football. Caray began broadcasting baseball for the Tulsa Oilers of the Southern League in 1963, and also announced for the minor league Atlanta Crackers. He joined the NBA's St. Louis Hawks broadcasting team in 1967, moving to Atlanta with the franchise the following year.

Over his career, Caray was recognized with six Georgia Sportscaster-of-the Year awards from the National Sportswriters and Sportscasters Association, as well as a Georgia-area Emmy.

An eight-time winner of the Georgia Sportscaster of the Year Award from the National Sportswriters and Sportscasters Association, Van Wieren served as play-by-play announcer for the Atlanta Hawks on TBS from 1991-94. Beginning in 1986, he also worked NBA games for TNT and TBS.

Van Wieren joined TBS in 1975. He covered the Atlanta Flames of the National Hockey League, the Hawks, and Atlanta Falcons preseason football, and also served as a sports reporter for CNN. In 1985-86, Van Wieren served as play-by-play announcer for TBS Sports' coverage of Big 10 Conference college football games.

In 2004, both Caray and Van Wieren were inducted into the Atlanta Braves Hall of Fame.

Caray, after a long series of illnesses, passed away toward the end of the 2008 season. Former Braves star Mark Lemke had been subbing for Caray as Van Wieren's broadcast partner during Braves' road-game broadcasts. And after the 2008 season, Van Wieren announced his retirement.

LET'S DON'T FORGET:

Walter Victor. The longtime photographer of the Atlanta Braves, Victor has photographed virtually every major sporting event in the city. He became the official team photographer when the franchise moved from Milwaukee to Atlanta in 1966, and became an institution with the team.

Victor saw 33 months of combat in World War II, and participated in such events as the D-Day landing on Normandy and the liberation of Dachau, one of Nazi Germany's most notorious death camps. He won the Bronze Star, and parachuted behind enemy lines during the D-Day invasion. When the war ended, Victor returned home to his family and took a job as a mechanic at the U.S. Army depot in Forest Park. He worked there for 30 years, and later took a sideline job as photographer for the Braves, and then later, the Atlanta Falcons.

CLINTON DILLARD CASTLEBERRY, JR.

Castleberry's No. 19 jersey remains the only one ever retired by the Georgia Tech football program. Despite playing only one season for Tech as a freshman in 1942, his legend remains strong in Atlanta.

Atlanta Boy's High School best all-around athlete from 1939-41, Castleberry was an All-State halfback in 1940; All-State and All-Southern in 1941; All-State basketball guard in 1941; and All-State baseball outfielder in 1942. As a running back at Atlanta Boy's, the 5-9, 155-pound Castleberry averaged 171 yards a game and scored 102 points.

Castleberry was a Georgia Tech All-American and All-SEC performer in 1942, and led Tech to a 9-2 record, as well as a Cotton Bowl berth that year. During a year in which freshmen were ruled eligible to play varsity ball since rosters were so drained by the war, Castleberry showed spectacular prowess in games against Navy (where his key role in the 21-0 romp was broadcast nationwide and to the Armed Forces on radio) and Notre Dame (which Tech beat for the first time in South Bend with Castleberry's help) before his knee was injured in a hard-fought Florida game.

Despite the injury, which forced him to play only sparingly the rest of the season and in the Cotton Bowl, he finished in the top three in Heisman trophy voting as a freshman. Many assumed he would win it in the next season or two.

But Castleberry joined the Army Air Corps the following year. And on Election Day 1944, Castleberry flew on a B-26 Marauder from Nigeria into Senegal. The plane was never seen again. Sixteen days later and after an extensive search, on Nov. 23, 1944, the army officially changed the serviceman's classification from "Missing In Action" to "Killed, No Body."

Many servicemen, having heard that GT-Navy game and knowing of his sacrifice, would later take pride in saying "Castleberry was here."

Among the many trophies and recognitions named for Castleberry is the Castleberry Award, presented to an outstanding high school student athlete by the Atlanta Touchdown Club.

LET'S DON'T FORGET:

Leon Hardeman. Member of the 1952 Georgia Tech National Championship team ... First-team All-SEC in 1952 ... All-SEC 1951 (AP 3rd team, UPI 2nd team) and 1953- (AP 2nd team, UPI 2nd team) ... MVP of the 1953 Sugar Bowl ... Scored 22 TDs and rushed for 1,794 yards (5.3 per carry) during his Yellow Jacket career ... Played on Orange and two Sugar Bowl championship teams ... Member of the Georgia Tech Hall of Fame.

William Raymond Healy. Consensus All-American lineman at Georgia Tech in 1948 (selected 1st team by four different services) ... Named the SEC's Most Valuable Player as a lineman in 1948 by the Birmingham Quarterback Club and the SEC Lineman of the Year by the Atlanta Touchdown Club ... Helped lead the Yellow Jackets to a combined record of 17-4-0 as a junior and senior ... Named to All-Southern teams in 1941 and 1942 at the Baylor School of Chattanooga ... Awarded the Bronze and Silver stars for bravery during World War II.

AL CIRALDO

The radio voice of Georgia Tech football and basketball for nearly four decades, Ciraldo called 416 football and 1,030 basketball games.

Ciraldo's signature expression "toe meets leather" began signaling the start of Tech football games in 1954. Although Ciraldo stepped away from Georgia Tech play-by-play duties before the 1992 season, he continued to host the pre-game and halftime broadcasts.

Ciraldo graduated from the University of Florida with a degree in radio broadcasting in 1948 and came to Atlanta in 1949. Until 1948, he studied in the University of Florida and received his degree in media. That same year he arrived on the Atlanta scene.

Ciraldo had a longtime sports love affair with Atlanta. With WGLS in Decatur he did high school sports and at WBGE he did high school football and. In 1954, Ciraldo came to Tech and WGST. After 30 years with WGST, Ciraldo moved to WCNN-AM in 1984.

What They've Said: *"Everyone knows how much Al Ciraldo meant to Georgia Tech, but he has meant so much to Bobby Cremins as well. As far as I'm concerned, he's a legend and a part of Georgia Tech that can never be replaced."*
— Bobby Cremins

LET'S DON'T FORGET:

Hank Morgan. Known as "Hank the Prank ..." Began covering the Crackers on the radio in 1954 ... He called the games, kept records on players and used his imagination to generate widespread interest in the Crackers ... Recreated numerous Cracker road games from his closet-sized radio booth, using sound effects such as crowd noise, bats cracking balls, etc.

NATALIE COHEN

Playing competitive tennis for 73 years, Cohen won 13 Georgia State Women's Open Doubles Championships. At the age of 42, she won both the Atlanta City and Georgia State women's singles and doubles championships, equivalent to the state's Grand Slam. Cohen was the first woman to chair an NCAA men's tennis championship and the first Southern woman to chair a match at Forrest Hills in the U.S. Tennis Championships.

And for more than 50 years Cohen was a certified tennis official, serving as linesman, umpire and referee for the city of Atlanta, state of Georgia, Southeastern regional, NCAA and professional tournaments.

Cohen was born and raised in Atlanta, and attended Fraser Street and Inman elementary schools, Bass Junior High School and Girls' High School. When she was eight, her father began taking her to football games at the University of Georgia, his alma mater. Cohen became so enamored with the game that she decided to attend a college that had a respectable football team, ending up at the University of California.

Cohen began playing competitive tennis at age eight and when she stopped at age 81 she had more than earned the title of "Atlanta's First Lady of Tennis." Of her 43-year career as a tennis umpire, she said, "I liked to officiate in tournaments where there was a minimum of uptight players and prima donnas. I preferred to be around people who enjoyed the game."

Cohen was known as an adamant booster of her alma mater's Golden Bears. At age 74, she delivered a fiery pep talk to the team during halftime of a game with the school's arch rival, Sanford. The team came back to overcome an eight-point deficit and upset the heavily favored Indians, 17-11. She also has a seat dedicated in her honor in the school's football stadium - section RR, Seat 1, the "Natalie Cohen" seat.

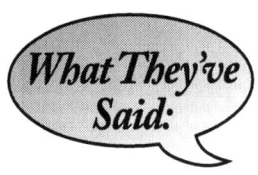

"I was giving a clinic one day to some young players and I asked them, 'When was the last time any of you asked a friend to play just for the fun of it?' I got a blank stare from the entire group ... We need to teach kids to enjoy the game first and understand that every time someone goes on the court one will win and one will lose. Lessons in how to accept loss should be as important as how to hit a backhand."

— Natalie Cohen

THOMAS G. COUSINS

The man who brought professional ice hockey south of the Mason-Dixon Line has left a long and distinguished sports legacy that is as notable as the imprints he made on Atlanta's skyline.

After graduating from the Darlington School in Rome, GA, in 1948, the University of Georgia in 1952 and serving in the U.S. Air Force, Cousins founded Cousins Properties Inc. in 1958. Thus began a career in commercial real estate that would make Cousins one of Atlanta's wealthiest and most influential men.

Cousins was front and center during some of the city's biggest growth periods, and in 1972, signed the paychecks when the NHL expanded to Atlanta into an arena he helped build, the Omni.

However, by the late 1970s, after years of poor playoff performances, declining attendance and a bad economy, Cousins was forced to sell the Flames to a Canadian businessman, who relocated them to Calgary.

But Cousins' imprint on the city's sports scene remains much deeper than Atlanta's first attempt to host an NHL franchise. A lifelong golf enthusiast, Cousins developed the first golf courses centered in residential communities in Atlanta including Indian Hills, Hidden Hills, Cross Creek and Big Canoe. In addition, he was one of the 25 original founders of the Atlanta Country Club, the site of more than 30 PGA events, a U.S. Women's Amateur, and a U.S. Senior Amateur.

In 1987, Cousins formed the Cousins Foundation and funded it with Cousins Properties stock. Through his foundation, he has given millions of dollars to various causes but none speaks louder to Cousins' desire to use real estate to make the world a better place to live than the East Lake project.

The East Lake community, located east of downtown Atlanta, used to be one of the city's wealthiest neighborhoods. Atlanta Sports Legend Bobby Jones' home course was located in the community, the East Lake Country Club. But the neighborhood changed in the 1960s when the U.S. government built a public housing project. Drugs, crime and lower property values followed.

(Continued on next page)

THOMAS G. COUSINS

The Cousins Foundation, along with the federal government and Atlanta Housing Authority, set about to renovate the area. To date, the foundation has committed more than $25 million to the project, and the end result is a neighborhood literally brought back from the dead. In 1998, the PGA championship was played at East Lake, and it also hosted the 2002 U.S. Amateur. East Lake Golf Club is the permanent home of THE TOUR Championship presented by Coca-Cola. The Club also hosted THE TOUR Championship in 1998, 2000, 2002, 2004, 2005, 2006 and 2007. Beginning in 2007, THE TOUR Championship presented by Coca-Cola became part of the Playoffs for the FedExCup.

Cousins also was a member of the Augusta National Golf Club; the Cypress Point Club; the East Lake Golf Club; the National Golf Links of America; the Peachtree Golf Club; the Seminole Golf Club; The Honors Course; and The Royal and Ancient Golf Club.

What They've Said:

"I don't think anyone other than Tom could have pulled off the East Lake project. He's just gifted with a natural ability to do deals. People want to do business with him. Maybe it's because his vision is so simple. He really just wants to improve the quality of life for his fellow man."

— Richard Courts, longtime friend and business associate

ROBERT EDWARD "BOBBY" COX

The Atlanta Braves all-time winningest manager, Cox had perhaps his best managerial season in 2005.

Or 2004. Or 2003. Or ... You get the idea.

Year after year, baseball pundits throughout the nation repeat the same sentiment, that Cox has managed to pull off the seemingly impossible: pulling together a group of A.) over-the-hill veterans; B.) wet-behind-the-ears rookies; C.) suspect starting pitching; D.) suspect bullpen pitching; E.) an injury riddled roster or F.) all of the above, and turn them into winners.

Specifically, winners of 14 consecutive division titles, a record unmatched by any other professional sports franchise in any other sport. Period.

The Braves' remarkable run of championship baseball began in 1991, one year after Cox returned to the dugout for his second managerial stint with the team. From 1978-81, Cox's first tenure in the Braves dugout, he compiled a 266-323 record and laid the groundwork for the club's National League West title in 1982.

Cox then began a four-year stint the Toronto Blue Jays' manager in 1982, lifting an habitual last-place team to within one game of attaining a World Series berth in 1985. In 1982, Cox led the Blue Jays to a 78-84 mark, the best record in their then-six-year existence. Toronto improved to 89-73 each of the next two seasons and won the AL East crown by going 99-62 in 1985.

Braves owner (and fellow Atlanta Sports Legend) Ted Turner lured Cox back to Atlanta as general manager in 1985, where he oversaw a farm system which set the foundation for the big-league club's future success. Cox took over field managing responsibilities on June 22, 1990, then devoted all his time to those duties when the Braves named fellow Atlanta Sports Legend John Schuerholz general manager later that year.

The Braves performance in 1991, when they went from worst-to-first and participated in one of history's most dramatic World Series, earned Cox several postseason honors. Among others, the Associated Press named him Major League Manager of the Year. Cox became the first manager to earn that honor in both leagues, having also won it with the Blue Jays in '85. In 1993, the Braves won a then-franchise record 104 games and became the first National League West team to win three straight divisional titles.

Cox has been named manager of the year six times by *The Sporting News;* no other manager has won the award more than three times since the magazine started the balloting in 1936.

In 2004, Cox earned his 200th career victory with a 6-4 decision over the New York Mets, becoming just the ninth skipper in big league history to reach that lofty milestone.

The Braves have won more games in the past 15 years than any other team in baseball. Their 2005 first-place finish was the 15th in a row for Cox in seasons in which he has managed from the outset, including his final year in Toronto in 1985.

(Continued on next page)

ROBERT EDWARD "BOBBY" COX

The Sporting News named Cox the National League manager of the year for the second straight season in 2003 as he moved past Casey Stengel into ninth place on the all-time managerial win list. He joined the Yankees Joe McCarthy as the only managers in major league history to guide their teams to 100 or more wins in a season six times.

Cox spent seven years in the Los Angeles Dodgers farm system before being acquired by Atlanta late in 1966. After playing in 1967 for AAA Richmond, he was traded to the New York Yankees and beat out Mike Ferraro, the Yankees outstanding spring training rookie, for the third base job in 1968. Cox made the Topps Rookie All-Star team that season, but lost his job to roommate Bobby Murcer in '69.

Bad knees forced Cox to retire as a player at age 30. He was appointed manager of the Yankees Class-A Fort Lauderdale club in 1971. His teams never finished lower than fourth in his six seasons in the Yankees system. After serving as the Yankees first base coach in 1977, Cox moved south to manage the Braves.

Cox was among the inaugural class of inductees into the Atlanta Sports Hall of Fame.

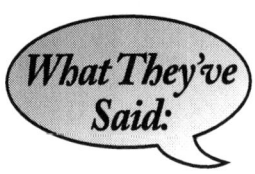

"I can't thank Bobby Cox enough for what he's done for my career and this organization. To this day, I still don't know how he does it. He kept sticking guys out there and giving them confidence."

— Chipper Jones, Atlanta Braves

BY THE NUMBERS

MANAGERIAL RECORD

Year	Lg	Div	Team	G	W	L	Pct	Finish
1978	NL	West	Atlanta	162	69	93	.426	6th place
1979	NL	West	Atlanta	160	66	94	.412	6th place
1980	NL	West	Atlanta	161	81	80	.503	4th place
1981	NL	West	Atlanta	55	25	29	.463	4th place
1981	NL	West	Atlanta	52	25	27	.481	5th place
1982	AL	East	Toronto	162	78	84	.481	6th place
1983	AL	East	Toronto	162	89	73	.549	4th place
1984	AL	East	Toronto	163	89	73	.549	2nd place
1985	AL	East	Toronto	161	99	62	.615	1th place
1990	NL	West	Atlanta	97	40	57	.412	6th place
1991	NL	West	Atlanta	162	94	68	.580	1st place
1992	NL	West	Atlanta	162	98	64	.605	1st place
1993	NL	West	Atlanta	162	104	58	.642	1st place
1994	NL	East	Atlanta	114	68	46	.596	2nd place (strike year)
1995	NL	East	Atlanta	144	90	54	.625	1st place (World Championship)
1996	NL	East	Atlanta	162	96	66	.593	1st place
1997	NL	East	Atlanta	162	101	61	.623	1st place
1998	NL	East	Atlanta	162	106	56	.654	1st place
1999	NL	East	Atlanta	162	103	59	.636	1st place
2000	NL	East	Atlanta	162	95	67	.586	1st place
2001	NL	East	Atlanta	162	88	74	.543	1st place
2002	NL	East	Atlanta	161	101	59	.631	1st place
2003	NL	East	Atlanta	162	101	61	.623	1st place
2004	NL	East	Atlanta	162	96	66	.593	1st place
2005	NL	East	Atlanta	162	90	72	.556	1st place
2006	NL	East	Atlanta	162	79	83	.488	3rd place
2007	NL	East	Atlanta	162	84	78	.519	3rd place
2008	NL	East	Atlanta	162	72	90	.444	4th place

LET'S DON'T FORGET:

Bobby Dews. A member of the Braves organization as a manager, coach, instructor or administrator since 1975 ... Finished seventh season as Braves bullpen coach in 2005 ... Worked in Atlanta under Bobby Cox as a bullpen coach in 1979; third base coach in 1980-81; first base coach under manager Eddie Haas; and third base coach for Bobby Wine in 1985 ... Previously served as the Braves minor league field coordinator ... Succeeded Hank Aaron as director of player development in December 1989 ... A roving minor league instructor in 1986 and 1987 ... Manager of Class-A Greenwood of the Western Carolinas League in 1975, Dews spent eight of the next 11 years managing in the Braves system, guiding five of his clubs to their respective playoffs ... AA Savannah Braves, who won the Southern League championship in 1978, earned Dews manager of the year honors ... Graduated from Edison, GA, High School and attended Georgia Tech, where he was a standout basketball and baseball player ... Earned a degree in English from West Georgia College in 1968 ... An accomplished writer, Dews had a novel, *Largo*, published in 1986 and his book *Legends, Demons and Dreams* was published in 2004.

JIM CRAIG

Although he will always be remembered as the goaltender who played a central role in what was arguably the 20th century's biggest sports story, the highlight of Craig's professional career occurred in Atlanta.

Craig was between the pipes for the 1980 U.S. Olympic hockey team, a group of scrappy, all-American kids who captured the nation's imagination. In the Lake Placid, NY, Winter Olympics, and during a time of what then-President Jimmy Carter called a national "crisis of confidence," Craig and his team upset the mighty Soviet Olympic hockey dynasty, and eventually went on to win the gold medal. Literally overnight, Craig, Head Coach Herb Brooks, and the rest of the squad were genuine, bona fide American heroes.

Almost immediately after the Games were over, the team went their own separate ways, and Craig's path led him to Atlanta. The Flames were in the middle of what would be their final season in the South; poor playoff performances, a sour economy and low attendance were fueling rumors that the team would be sold and relocated elsewhere, most likely, Calgary, Alberta, Canada.

But the Flames owned Craig's NHL rights, and six nights after winning the gold medal against Finland, Craig found himself in a white and red, gold-trimmed Atlanta Flames sweater, against the Colorado Rockies. That night, Craig stopped 24 of the 25 shots he faced, leading the Flames to a 4-1 victory before a rare sellout crowd at the Omni.

It would prove to be the highlight of his star-crossed NHL career.

Craig saw action in only four games for the rest of the season, suffering from an ulcer and exhaustion. He was traded to the Boston Bruins for the 1980-81 season. Boston wanted to send him to the minors to work on his technique - Craig had trouble handling the puck away from the net - but he resisted the demotion. The Bruins relented, and made him the No. 3 goaltender in a league where two goalies are the norm.

Craig was finding that his status as an American hero didn't mean a thing in the National Hockey League, which was heavily dominated by Canadian players.

The following summer, he broke his right index finger while training with Team USA for the Canada Cup. When he reported to Boston, the Bruins promptly sent him to their Erie, PA, AHL affiliate for more seasoning. He soon returned to Boston when a lump was discovered on his shoulder. The lump turned out to be benign, but while recovering from surgery Craig fell off a ladder while working at his home, breaking a bone in his ankle. He finally reported to Erie late in 1981-82, but was quickly sidelined with back spasms after an on-ice collision.

With his NHL career seemingly suck in neutral, the Bruins advised Craig to contact other teams regarding a possible deal, but Craig found no interest. His professional career ended with a brief stint with the Minnesota North Stars in 1983-84.

Nothing can diminish the magnitude of Craig's accomplishments in the 1980 Winter Olympics. And his appearance in Atlanta, and the excitement which it generated, earned him a place in the city's sports history.

"We were just a bunch of talented, dedicated, wonderful guys who believed in one goal, and stuck all of their own personal ambitions away to achieve it. If that's a miracle, I believe in that."

— Jim Craig

LET'S DON'T FORGET:

Phil Myre and Dan Bouchard. One of the NHL's most solid goaltending tandems of the early to mid 1970s ... Joined the team together as the Flames first- and second-round expansion draft choices ... Helped lead the Flames to the NHL playoffs in only the franchise's second year, an NHL record at the time ... Split time equally between the goal posts during their four years together with the franchise ... Bouchard remains the all-time winningest goaltender while the franchise was in Atlanta.

Manon Rheaume. The first woman to ever play in a professional ice hockey game ... On Sept. 23, 1992, the goaltender suited up for the NHL's Tampa Bay Lightning for a preseason game ... The IHL Atlanta Knights, a farm team for Tampa Bay, signed her to a contract ... Made history on Dec. 13, 1992, when she played in an Atlanta Knights regular season game.

WAYMAN CREEL

Georgia's fifth all-time winningest high school coach, Creel enjoyed a record of 315-105-12 as head football coach at Atlanta's Northside, Lakeside and Westminster high schools. That record makes his eighth on the all-time national list for victories.

Creel coached 39 years at three high schools and was head coach at Westminster during the final seven seasons of his career, where he won three state championships and one national coach of the year award.

Creel coached at Northside (1951-69), Lakeside (1970-82) and Westminster (1983-1989). His state titles came at Northside in 1957 and Lakeside in 1970 and 1972. In 1977, he was presented with the national Coach of the Year award by the National High School Athletic Coaches Association.

A former fullback at Richardson High (now College Park High), Creel went to Georgia on a football scholarship, but his college career was interrupted in 1943 by World War II. After the war, he became an assistant at North Fulton before starting the Northside football program in 1951. His first win came against North Fulton.

Creel was transferred to Washington High in an effort to racially balance the faculties at Atlanta public schools. But he never coached a game there and switched to Lakeside in DeKalb County. And it was there that his true coaching legacy began. He won state championships in two of his first three years with rosters that at times exceeded 100 players. In his final season at Lakeside (1982), he surpassed Valdosta's Wright Bazemore as the winningest coach in Georgia high school history.

After his 13th season at Lakeside, he left the public school system and moved to Westminster. He took the Wildcats to the playoffs for three straight seasons, once losing to Lakeside. In 1987, he gained his 300th coaching victory by beating Chamblee.

Creel also served two terms as the president of the Georgia Athletic Coaches Association. He died in 2003 at the age of 64.

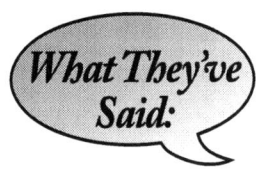

"I had great relationships with some great coaches like Vince Dooley and Erk Russell, but nobody was a better leader of men than Coach Creel."

— Buzzy Rosenberg, who played for Creel at Northside in the late 1960s and later was an All-SEC defensive back and punt returner at Georgia

BOBBY CREMINS

Under Cremins, Georgia Tech went from collegiate basketball doormat to perennial contender, a force to be reckoned with in a tradition-rich conference.

Cremins was born on July 4, 1947, in New York's Bronx, where he earned the nickname "the basketball kid of Southern Boulevard." He became a basketball standout under the legendary coach Frank McGuire at the University of South Carolina, where he earned his bachelor's degree in marketing and his master's in guidance and counseling. A three-year starter for USC at point guard, Cremins led the Gamecocks to one of their most successful seasons. South Carolina was 25-3 (14-0 in ACC) during his 1969-70 senior season.

After graduation, Cremins spent one year playing professional basketball in Ecuador before beginning his collegiate coaching career in 1971 at Point Park College in Pittsburgh. He returned to his alma mater for a two-year stint as an assistant coach to McGuire in 1972. He then moved to Appalachian State, where he became the youngest Division I head coach in the NCAA.

Cremins assumed the head coaching position at Georgia Tech before the 1981-82 season, at a time when many thought that the Ramblin Wreck could never compete equally with its ACC neighbors. He came to a school that, in its first two years of ACC competition in 1980 and '81, notched a cumulative 12-41 record, 1-29 in league competition. Some Tech fans attended games wearing paper bags over their heads. A section of 2,000 seats at Alexander Memorial Coliseum often sat empty, purchased by fans at other schools so they could qualify for ACC Tournament tickets.

But by the time Cremins stepped aside after the 2000 season, Tech had made 10 NCAA appearances, including nine straight from 1985 through 1993, and enjoyed a fearsome home court advantage. The 1990 squad reached the Final Four for the first and only time in school history. The Jackets tied for first place in the ACC in '85 and finished alone atop the standings in 1996. They won a trio of ACC titles - in '85, '90 and '93 - and posted 13 consecutive winning seasons and 15 in Cremins' 19 years on the job.

Cremins was thrice voted ACC coach of the year ('83, '85, '96), a total exceeded only by two Hall of Fame coaches, North Carolina's Dean Smith and Duke's Mike Krzyzewski. In 1990, he was named Naismith National Coach of the Year. Cremins' program produced the ACC player of the year in 1990 in Dennis Scott; eight rookies of the year in the 14 seasons from 1983 through '96; 13 first team All-ACC selections; and a dozen first-round NBA draft choices. Perhaps no one in the 50-year history of ACC basketball ranks as a greater program builder.

Cremins is a member of the Atlanta Sports Hall of Fame. In 2006, he returned to coaching at the College of Charleston.

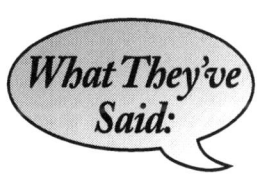
What They've Said:

"Bobby was a very good coach. He was a heck of a recruiter and one of the finest persons I ever worked with. He was always upbeat. He was a fighter."

— Homer Rice, retired Tech athletics director

BILL CURRY

A native of College Park, GA, Curry brought his NFL Super Bowl experiences back to his Georgia Tech alma mater as head football coach, and later ascended to the nation's top collegiate coaching job at the University of Alabama.

Today, he may face his greatest professional challenge ever, building a collegiate football program from scratch.

Curry played linebacker for Georgia Tech and lettered from 1962-64. He captained the Yellow Jackets his senior season, and his overall playing career was part of a 21-9-1 record. In 1991, he was chosen as a member of Tech's All-Time Team.

As a pro, Curry played for the Green Bay Packers in 1965-66, and helped the Packers defeat the Dallas Cowboys, 34-27, for the NFC Championship title, played in the Cotton Bowl in Texas. The Packers defeated the Kansas City Chiefs 35-10 in Super Bowl I. Two years later, as a member of the legendary Baltimore Colts, Curry was an eyewitness when another legendary team, the Joe Namath-led New York Jets, defeated his heavily favored 15-1 Colts in Super Bowl III, by a final score of 16-7.

Curry won a second Super Bowl title in the championship's game fifth installment, when the Colts defeated the Dallas Cowboys 16-13. In 1970, he helped lead the Colts to a 27-17 AFC title victory over the Oakland Raiders, but lost to the Miami Dolphins in the 1971 AFC title game, 21-0. Curry's pro career finished in 1974, after spending one year with the Houston Oilers and then the Los Angeles Rams. He was selected to the Associated Press All-Pro second-team in 1970 and was chosen a first-team All-AFL pick in 1971 and 1972 by United Press International.

Curry spent one year as an assistant coach at Tech in 1976, before returning to the Green Bay Packers as an offensive line coach 1977-79. He returned to Georgia Tech as head coach from 1980-86, where his record of 31-43-4 nonetheless produced some memorable moments for Tech football fans.

Curry led Tech to a 3-3 tie against No. 1-ranked Notre Dame in 1980 and a victory at fourth-ranked Alabama in 1981, as well as back-to-back victories over nationally ranked Georgia teams in 1984-85. The Jackets also earned their first ACC victory in 1983, a 20-10 win over North Carolina State. Tech scored an upset of 13th-ranked Clemson in 1984 that ended the Tigers 20-game ACC winning streak.

In 1985, Curry was named ACC Coach of the Year, when he led Tech to a 9-2-1 record, including a 5-1 mark in the ACC. That year, he guided the Jackets to a victory over heavily favored Michigan State in the 1985 All-American Bowl for Tech's first bowl victory in more than a decade.

Curry, briefing the media on Georgia State's new football program

Curry took over the program at the University of Alabama from 1987-89, and then as head coach at the University of Kentucky from 1990-96. In 2008, he was hired as Georgia State University's first-ever football coach, when GSU's season in the Colonial Athletic Conference begins in 2010.

BY THE NUMBERS

PLAYING CAREER
1963-1964 Georgia Tech
1965-1966 Green Bay Packers
1967-1972 Baltimore Colts
1973 Houston Oilers
1974 Los Angeles Rams

COACHING CAREER
1980-1986 Georgia Tech
1987-1989 Alabama
1990-1996 Kentucky
2008-present Georgia State

LET'S DON'T FORGET:

Frank Broyles. Born in Atlanta ...Led the Arkansas Razorbacks to one national championship and seven Southwest Conference titles ... Served as head coach at Missouri and assistant coach at Baylor, Florida and Georgia Tech ... 1944 All-American at Georgia Tech ... Two-time All-SEC ... Three-year Georgia Tech football letterman

Hal M. Miller. Co-captain of the 1952 Georgia Tech National Championship team selected by International News Service ... Selected by four news services as an All-American in 1952 ... 1952 All-SEC first team (Associated Press) and second team (United Press International) ... 1951 All-SEC third team (Associated Press) ... Tech compiled a 23-0-1 overall record and captured two SEC titles with a 13-0 mark from 1951-52 with Miller at offensive tackle ... Captured bowl victories over Baylor (17-14) in the 1952 Orange and Mississippi (24-7) in the 1953 Sugar Bowl.

BOBBY DODD

One of only two men enshrined in the College Football Hall of Fame both as a player and a coach (the other being Amos Alonzo Stagg), Dodd is the greatest head football coach in Georgia Tech history, compiling a 165-64-8 mark from 1945-1966, and leading the Yellow Jackets to the 1952 National Championship. He won six bowl games and two SEC titles, and had a 31-game winning streak from 1951-1953.

Dodd was born in 1908 in Galax, VA. He was named after another famous Virginian, Confederate General Robert E. Lee. Early in the fall of 1921, the Dodd family relocated to Kingsport, TN. The young Bob Dodd, 12 years old and weighing only 100 pounds, made the seventh-grade team of Kingsport's first organized football program.

From 1924-26, the Kingsport Indians would ride a high wave of success. They were helped by Dodd, who moved from a receivers' position to quarterback and kicker, gaining two state titles. In 1926, Dodd was admitted with a scholarship to the University of Tennessee at Knoxville. He had considered coming to Atlanta to attend Georgia Tech, but his brother John dissuaded him, warning that he was "too dumb to go [there]." He also considered attending the University of Georgia but could not gain a scholarship.

At Tennessee, Dodd played four years under Bob Neyland, enjoying great success as an all-American. He became a starter in the fourth game of his sophomore season, 1928, in which he threw a touchdown pass to tie Alabama, 13-13. Then he punted out of bounds inside the Alabama 1-yard line and Tennessee got a safety on the next play to win, 15-13. In the 26 games Dodd started, Tennessee won 24, lost 1, and tied 1. He was named to legendary sportswriter Grantland Rice's All-American team in 1930.

In 1931, Dodd accepted the job of assistant backfield coach under Coach William Alexander at Georgia Tech, where he would stay for the rest of his life.

Tech's 1931 football program suffered its worst record since 1902: 2-7-1. Things were so bad that in 1931 the Athletic Association could not pay the coaches' salaries. Dodd and another assistant coach were paid out of Alexander's own pocket during these hard times.

In 1944, Alexander retired and Dodd rose to the position of head coach, where he would remain for the next 21 years.

Dodd believed in short, non-contact practices because he didn't want his players to get bored or stale and he insisted that they spend more time studying than practicing. Dodd was fond of telling parents, "We're not miracle workers, but if you send us a good boy to Georgia Tech, we will send you a good boy home."

Dodd retired as head coach in 1966 to serve another 10 years as director of the Athletic Association, where he retired in 1976 to act as an Alumni Association consultant until his death in 1988.

"[Bobby Dodd] taught us to care because he cared... he taught us that honesty is sacred, is absolute, and is eternal."
— Frank Broyles

LET'S DON'T FORGET:

Wade T. Mitchell. A solid quarterback for Dodd during Georgia Tech's dominating run in the 1950s ...During his four-year (1953-56) collegiate football career, Tech fashioned a 37-7-2 record ... The Yellow Jackets won four consecutive bowl games (1953 Sugar, 1954 Cotton, 1955 Sugar, 1956 Gator) ... Mitchell played in 43 career games, accounted for 1,352 yards of total offense threw eight TDs and rushed for seven more ... Named the 1956 Gator Bowl MVP...Scored Tech's second TD in the 1954 Cotton Bowl that secured the victory against Arkansas ... Standout athlete at North Fulton High School in football, track, swimming and basketball ... Led North Fulton basketball to the state title as team captain in 1953.

Johnny G. "Stumpy" Thomason. Three-year football letterman at Georgia Tech and two-year All-Southern Conference selection ... Helped lead Tech to the 1928 Rose Bowl championship ... Played in the pros for Brooklyn and Philadelphia ... Member of the Georgia Tech Hall of Fame ... Star athlete at Tech High School.

R.L. "SHORTY" DOYAL

A legendary coach at Atlanta's Boys High, "Shorty" Doyal had one of the best high school football coaching records in the nation during his 29-year career. Doyal's teams compiled a record of 234 wins, 59 losses, and 15 ties. During his tenure at Atlanta Boy's High School, he became Georgia's first 200-game winner. His teams there compiled a record of 200 victories, winning six southern championships, 10 state championships, and 13 city championships.

Doyal's teams won 34 consecutive games from 1933-36 and another 31 consecutive games from 1939-42. He completed his career at The Marist School where he coached his teams to another 34 wins, 18 losses, and 3 ties.

Founder of the North Georgia Football Coaches Association, Doyal was one of the early pioneers in establishing the high standards of Georgia high school athletics.

Doyal produced a string of great players who went on to star in college, including another Atlanta Sports Legend, Clint Castleberry, who became an All-American at Georgia Tech and later was killed in World War II.

CHARLES G. "LEFTY" DRIESELL

The beloved "Lefty" Driesell is the only coach in college basketball history to have won 100 games at four schools - Davidson, Maryland, James Madison, and a school that had never truly been known for its athletic prowess, Georgia State University.

Driesell ranks fourth all-time among college basketball coaches with 786 career wins. He enjoyed 22 seasons of 20 or more wins, and shares the NCAA record of taking four different schools to NCAA Tournament. He also won conference coach of the year in four different leagues (another NCAA record), and coached teams to four different conference tournament titles.

Driesell, left, with Dave Cohen

Driesell spent 41 years in coaching, and had the fifth-most wins in Division I history. His overall record of 786-394 gives him a .666 winning percentage. He went 176-65 at Davidson from 1960-69; 348-159 at Maryland from 1969-86; 159-111 at James Madison from 1988-97, and 103-59 in five-plus seasons at Georgia State.

His winningest season was in 2000-01, when the Georgia State Panthers went 29-5 and upset Wisconsin in the NCAA tournament before hanging tough with Maryland - an eventual Final Four participant - until the final 10 minutes.

Driesell had a 97-15 coaching record in high school before moving to the college ranks, tallying his career coaching record to 879 wins. His massive influence on college basketball also was evidenced by the number of assistant coaches who went on to be head coaches, individuals who went on to win more than 2,500 games as head coaches, more than any other coach in NCAA history. More than 15 of those have compiled more than 2300 Division I wins, another NCAA record.

Of Driesell's 162 games coached in the state of Georgia, he won 101 of them, and never lost a game to another Peach State school.

One of Driesell's most innovative creations was "Midnight Madness," which he developed while at Maryland. "I was meeting with my staff and we were sitting and talking about practicing drills," said Driesell. "The NCAA told us we could start practice on October 15. Well, I said, 'That means we can start practicing one minute past midnight on the 14th, so let's get a jump on everybody.'" Getting a "jump" just meant having his players run a mile at midnight, simply so Driesell could say that he started about 15 hours before everyone else. The team then practiced at 3 p.m. Saturday, when other teams were typically meeting for the first time. Players embraced the idea.

(Continued on next page)

CHARLES G. "LEFTY" DRIESELL

What They've Said:

"He has built a winner everywhere he has ever been."
— Gary Williams, who succeeded Driesell at Maryland

BY THE NUMBERS
COACHING HISTORY

Season	School	W-L	Pct.
1960-69	Davidson	176-65	.730
1969-86	Maryland	348-159	.686
1988-97	James Madison	159-111	.593
1997-03	Georgia State	103-59	.636
CAREER (41 Seasons)		**786-394**	**.666**

Fourth all time in career wins; 22 seasons of 20 or more wins; 13 trips to the NCAA Tournament and eight NIT appearances; overall record of 22-20 in the postseason; went to eight straight postseasons at Maryland; went to five straight postseasons at James Madison.

LET'S DON'T FORGET:

Dave Cohen. The voice of Georgia State University sports for more than 25 years ... A true mainstay of Atlanta's often-turbulent sports broadcasting industry ... Survived eight coaches, seven athletic directors, hundreds of players and more than 700 games, mostly basketball and baseball ... The longest-tenured voice of a Division I sports team in the state ... In 2010, will add Panther football to his list of broadcasting credentials.

Amater Z. Traylor. Born in Atlanta, GA ... Two-time Morehouse College basketball All-American (1925 and '26) ... Helped lead Morehouse College to the 1923 national championship ... All-Southern Intercollegiate Athletic Conference selection four consecutive years .... Later served as the chairman for the Organizational Committee for Athletics of the Georgia Council of Black Principals in 1947 and was the executive secretary of the Georgia Interscholastic Athletic Conference from 1958-1966.

Bob Reinhart. One of the most successful basketball coaches in Atlanta ... Head coach at Decatur High School ... Coached at Georgia State University for nine seasons, 1985-86 through 1993-94 ... Overall record was 107-148 for a .420 winning percentage ... Led Georgia State to its first NCAA appearance in 1990-91, which was a loss to Arkansas in the Omni in the first round.

DAVID DUVAL

One of only two four-time Division I first-team All-Americans in Georgia Tech golf history, Duval was ranked No. 1 in the world in 1999.

Duval grew up the son of a golf pro, Bob Duval (who himself would go on to win on the Senior PGA Tour). Duval had a sterling junior golf career and, while at Tech, was twice named ACC Player of the Year.

Duval turned pro in 1993 and spent a couple seasons on the Nationwide Tour before earning his PGA Tour card in 1995. He had almost immediate success; although he didn't post his first victory for a while, he qualified for the 1996 Presidents Cup team and posted a 4-0 record.

Duval's breakout season was 1998, when he won four times, and led the tour in money and scoring. From 1997- 2001, Duval won 13 times, including one major, while spending some time ranked No. 1 in the world. He shot 59 in the final round of the 1999 Bob Hope Chrysler Classic.

But Duval slipped to 80th on the money list in 2002; 211th in 2003; and by late 2003 had dropped off the PGA Tour. He stayed away for eight months, not returning until the 2004 U.S. Open. There was much speculation about the source of Duval's problems, which led to many rounds in the 80s. Duval maintained the causes were physical. Making adjustments to deal with back pain, he'd altered his swing, and began losing confidence as his scores plummeted.

In late 2004, Duval played nine tournaments and made the cut in three - including one Top 20 finish – and appeared to be on the way back to regaining his status as one of golfing's best. Duval had a successful start to the 2006 PGA Tour season, making the cut in his first two tournaments, as well as a very respectable finish of T-16 at the U.S. Open Championship at Winged Foot Golf Club, where his second round 68 was good enough for a tie as the best round of the tournament. Despite not reaching the same heights in the remaining two majors of the year, his performances continued a general upward trend.

After a steady start to 2007 during the West Coast Swing, Duval once again disappeared from the tour. He later revealed that this was due to a difficult pregnancy his wife was going through. This prompted the PGA Tour to amend its medical exemption policies - and Duval was granted 20 starts for next season.

After a lackluster first half of the year, Duval reappeared on the leaderboard of The Open Championship. He shot 73-69-83-71 for the week and finished T-39.

Duvall, who attended Archer High School in Atlanta, was coached by Marian Armstrong-Perkins of David T. Howard High School. At age 15 she defeated the top prep-school sprinter in Atlanta. Her coach recommended McGuire for the summer clinic run by Ed Temple, coach of the very successful Tigerbelles at Tennessee State University in Nashville.

(Continued on next page)

DAVID DUVAL

BY THE NUMBERS

CAREER
PGA Tour wins - 13
Nationwide Tour - 1
PGA Tour lending money winner - 1998
Vanden Trophy - 1998
Byron Nelson Award - 1998

LET'S DON'T FORGET:

John Carson. All-state performer in golf, as well as football and basketball at Atlanta's Roosevelt High ... An Atlanta native ... Three-year letterman at the University of Georgia in football, basketball, baseball and golf ... Played in the NFL for the Washington Redskins from 1954-1960.

Bryce Molder. Along with Duval, Georgia Tech's only other four-time Division I first-team All-American in golf ... Two-time academic All-American ... Twice collegiate player of the year ... Twice a member of the Walker Cup team ... Three times a member of the Palmer Cup team ... Twice a quarterfinalist in the U.S. Amateur ... Low amateur at the U.S. Open in 2001.

EDITH MCGUIRE DUVALL

An Atlanta native, Duvall's track and field was short but spectacular, highlighted when she broke legendary runner Wilma Rudolph's 1960 record in the 200-meter sprint in the 1964 Tokyo Olympic Games.

Duvall captured gold that year in the 200 meters and the silver medal in the 100- and 400-meter relay in 1964. In the 200-meter final, she held off Poland's Irena Kirszenstein to take the gold medal. She added a third medal to her tally as a member of the American 4 x 100 meter relay team, which placed second to Poland.

Duvall is the only American woman to hold three different National Amateur Athletic Union (AAU) titles at different times. An AAU All-American from 1961-1966, she was undefeated in 1964 at 200 meters. She won six National AAU titles, including four outdoors, taking the 200-220 title in 1964 and 1965 and the 100 meters and long jump crowns in 1963. She also won two AAU indoor crowns at the 220 distance, and was the first woman to win the 100 and 200 meters and anchor the winning United States' 400-meter relay team in a meet against Russia.

In 1964, Duvall ranked fourth in the Sportswoman of the World competition and was among the 10 finalists for the James E. Sullivan Award, which honors the most outstanding amateur athlete in the United States.

Her awards since the 1960s were numerous as well. In 1991, she was a recipient of the NCAA Silver Anniversary Award for outstanding athletes who distinguished themselves in their careers. After graduating from Tennessee State University, Duvall toured East Africa for the U.S. State Department. She then served as an educator in Atlanta. She was also inducted into the U.S. Track & Field, Tennessee, and National Track Halls of Fame.

Born in Atlanta on June 3, 1944, Duvall was the youngest of four children. Her first experience with track and field was during her elementary school's May Day celebration.

In June 2009, she was inducted into the Atlanta Sports Hall of Fame.

BILL ELLIOTT

This racing legend built one of the most distinguished records in NASCAR Winston Cup history. In the process, Elliott, a native of Dawsonville (part of the metro Atlanta statistical area), turned his hometown into a hotbed of stock car activity and enterprise.

Beginning in 1976, Elliott – NASCAR's first million-dollar bonus winner - participated in almost 750 races, achieved 44 wins, collected 55 career poles, and amassed winnings of more than $70 million – all the while remaining true to his reputation as one of professional sports' most humble, approachable and endearing Atlanta Sports Legends.

Racing was a family affair during Elliott's childhood. Father George took his three sons, Ernie, Dan and Bill, to the racetrack on numerous occasions. The whole family was passionate about racing and it wasn't long before the Elliott boys were behind the wheel. During events at local tracks - like the Dixie Speedway in metro Atlanta - youngest son Bill demonstrated a raw, natural talent for the sport, rocketing around racetracks in record-setting fashions.

On Feb. 29, 1976, at North Carolina Speedway, the 20-year-old entered his first Winston Cup race. The Elliott family once struggled to pay the entry fees for their races, but now they were a fierce, ferocious force on the NASCAR circuit. Elliott won his first pole on April 10, 1981 at Darlington Raceway.

The family's racing operation got a financial boost in 1982 when a Michigan-based investor provided the funding needed to keep Elliott racing. That following year, Elliott began his first full season on the circuit. On Nov. 20, 1983, he found victory lane at Riverside International Raceway in his 117th Winston Cup race.

As the years sped past, Elliott could usually be found in the winner's circle. In 1985, he won 11 races and 11 poles on his way to winning the first Winston Million in NASCAR history, bringing a new fame to himself and the sport of auto racing. His victories in the Daytona 500, the Winston 500 at Talladega and the Southern 500 at Darlington earned him the million-dollar bonus and the nickname, "Million Dollar Bill."

Elliott's success also landed him in the pages *Sports Illustrated* as the first Winston Cup driver to appear on the cover. Additional glory followed and in 1988, with six wins, six poles, 11 top-five and 22 top-10 finishes in 29 races, Elliott earned NASCAR's Winston Cup championship.

In 1995, Elliott began his own team and assumed sole ownership a year later. In 2000, he celebrated his 25*th* anniversary in the NASCAR Winston Cup Series. Elliott proved he still had the moves of a champion when he captured the pole at one of the circuit's most famous races: the Daytona 500. He made history once again in his No. 9 Dodge Dealers Intrepid R/T when he won the pole and the race at Homestead-Miami Speedway on Nov. 11, 2001, Elliott's first victory since Sept. 4, 1994.

Elliott's 2001 standings were his best overall since 1994 with one win; two poles; five top-fives; nine top-10s; and a 15th-place finish in points. In the 2002 season, he won four poles; finished four times in the top five; 11 times in the top 10; and captured the checkered flag twice in a row - once at the Pennsylvania 500 and again at the Brickyard 400.

On Nov. 9, 2003, at Rockingham, Elliott moved up from a start in the rear of the field and led 140 of 393 laps in a dramatic victory. During that season, he also finished nine times in the top five and had 12 top-10 finishes. Moreover, Elliott achieved amazing popularity, winning the NMPA's "Most Popular Driver" Award a record 16 times, eventually retiring his name from the contest in 2003. In the 2005 NASCAR Cup season, Elliott raced a reduced driving schedule as he prepared to retire.

In 2008, Elliott was inducted into the Atlanta Sports Hall of Fame.

"Actually, I got my boys into racing because I wanted them to stay away from the back roads. If they were going to be driving fast, I wanted them to do it in the right place."

— George Elliott, father

BY THE NUMBERS

- One of only seven drivers to top $20 million in career winnings
- ESPN Speedweek's Fan Poll's "Driver of the Decade" for the 1980s
- Two-time winner: American "Driver of the Year" Award
- Two-time winner: Georgia Professional Athlete of the Year
- 1998 Georgia Sports Hall of Fame Inductee
- Named one of NASCAR's 50 Greatest Drivers of All Time in 1998
- Received the "Race Car Driving Legend Award" from the March of Dimes
- Four-time winner: American Auto Racing Writers and Broadcasters Association (AARWBA) All-America Team
- Jerry Titus Memorial Award: 1985
- National Motorsports Press Association Driver of the Year: 1985, 1986, 1987, 1988, 1991, 1992, 1993, 1994, 1995, 1996, 1997, 1998, 1999, 2000
- Auto Racing Digest Driver of the Year: 1985.
- McDonald's All-Star Race Team: 1991, 1992, 1993.
- Spirit of Ford Award: 2000

DOUGLAS LINTON "BUDDY" FOWLKES

A politician, an Atlanta fixture at City Hall for decades, and a devoted Georgia Tech advocate, Fowlkes was the only athlete to ever win high point honors in three SEC Track and Field championship meets, and set an SEC all-time individual high-point honors that stood for 33 years.

Over his Georgia Tech collegiate career, Fowlkes held the SEC Meet single-season record with 18 points, and won the SEC long jump title three times. His best college performances came with a 6-1$^{1/2}$ high jump; a 23.2 in the 220-yard low hurdles); a 23-11 in the long jump; a 20.8 time in the 220-yard run; and a 9.6 time in the 100-yard dash. And he ran a 9.5 in the 100-yard dash in the 1962 Georgia AAU meet at the age of 34.

After retiring from competition (and in between being elected and then re-elected numerous times to the Atlanta City Council), Fowlkes was named 1987 Outdoor Coach of the Year and 1985 NCAA Indoor (track) Coach of the Year for the Southeast region. As a Tech track coach, he oversaw the development of several Olympic and national champions, including Good Will Games and Olympic gold medalist Antonio McKay; Kevin Graham; Octavious Terry; Derek Mills; Uwezu McReynolds; and Derrick Adkins.

Fowlkes didn't start running track until he was a junior in high school. Two years earlier, while a freshman, he was diagnosed as having Osgood-Slaughter's disease that year. He had grown so fast, there was a growth the size of a walnut under each kneecap, and doctors told him he would never be able to play sports. By the time he graduated from North Fulton High, though, he was 6-foot-2 and had a Tech track scholarship in hand.

A year before being elected alderman, he had run the fastest 100 of his life - 9.5 seconds. A year after his election, at age 34, he ran another 9.5 and then retired. It was a world record for 34-year-olds, one that still stands.

What They've Said:

"Buddy was a very unusual athlete. There aren't many sprinters with his physique, but he was the best. I doubt anyone else his age could do the things he did as he got older. After he left us he gave remarkable performances in AAU meets. I think he has been one of the best track coaches we ever had in this section. I didn't stress track, didn't have enough money. But he took what he had and did an absolutely terrific job of coaching."

— Bobby Dodd

ALEXA STIRLING FRASER

Known as "the First Lady of East Lake" and "the Empress of Golf," Bobby Jones' childhood golfing partner won her first East Lake golf title at age 12. She would also win three National Women's Amateur Golf Championships in 1916 (at age 18!), 1919 and 1920, as well as the Canadian Open titles in 1920 and 1934.

Fraser was born in Atlanta on Sept. 5, 1897. Her nicknames matched Jones' "Emperor" moniker. Three days before her 19th birthday, she won the first of her three U.S. Women's Amateur Championships. When the tournament resumed after World War I, she successfully defended her crown in 1919 and '20, and placed second in that tournament in 1921, '23, and '25. Besides winning the Canadian Women's Open twice, she finished second in 1922 and 1925.

Fraser also was one of the Members of the Royal Ottawa's best golfers. She was made an honorary member in 1934 in recognition of her winning the Canadian Ladies Golf Association Championship for the second time. She also was Royal Ottawa ladies' champion nine times.

A member of the Georgia Golf Hall of Fame, Fraser returned to Atlanta for the 1976 U.S. Open shortly before her death. She died in Canada on April 15, 1977.

LET'S DON'T FORGET:

O.B. Keeler. An Atlanta newspaperman and close friend of Bobby Jones ... Traveled with Jones to tournaments and covered his career from start to finish, and would later describe Jones' career in two parts, "The Seven Lean Years and The Seven Fat Years" ... From 1916-23 Jones failed to win a major championship, losing in 10 straight before recording his first win. Following his disappointing showing at St. Andrews, while traveling to the 1921 U.S. Open later that year, Jones confided in Keeler, "I wonder if I'll ever win a championship?" Keeler responded, "Bobby, if you ever get it through your head that whenever you step out on the first tee of any competition, you are the best golfer in it, then you'll win this championship and a lot of others."

Harold Sargent. Brought the Ryder Cup to Atlanta in 1963 and the U.S. Open in 1976 ... Personally chosen by Bobby Jones to be the head pro at Atlanta Athletic Club's East Lake facility ... The Georgia PGA Pro of the Year in 1972.

WALT FRAZIER

With his Rolls Royce, flamboyant wardrobe and stylish fedora hats, Frazier was the toast of New York City as a member of the Knicks for 10 years. On the court, Frazier's quick hands on defense coupled with a cool demeanor earned him the nickname "Clyde."

Born in Atlanta and a graduate of David Howard High School (1959-63), Frazier was the cornerstone of Knick teams for a decade. He first caught the attention of pro scouts while playing at Southern Illinois University. A Division II All-America in 1964 and 1965 and a Division I All-America in 1967, Frazier led the Salukis to the 1967 NIT championship and was named MVP. During his career at Southern Illinois, Frazier was second-team All-American in 1967 by *The Sporting News*, and scored 884 points.

Frazier was the first-round choice of the Knicks in the 1967 draft, and earned All-Rookie honors. Frazier's play electrified crowds at Madison Square Garden. His offensive repertoire was a blend of smooth drives to the bucket and mid-range jump shots.

Even with an All-Star cast, Frazier led the Knicks in scoring five times. An adept passer, Frazier dished out 5,040 assists during his career (6.1 apg) and led the Knicks in assists 10 straight years. Many of those passes were directed to fellow Hall of Famers Willis Reed, Bill Bradley, Dave DeBusschere, Jerry Lucas and Earl "The Pearl" Monroe. Frazier, Reed, Bradley and DeBusschere copped the 1970 NBA title, and with the addition of Lucas and Monroe, the Knicks repeated in 1973.

Always the focal point of New York's offensive and defensive schemes, Frazier was named to the NBA's All-Defensive First Team seven times (1969-75), and selected to seven NBA All-Star Games (1970-76, MVP in the 1975 game). His NBA career totals include 15,581 points scored; 18.9 per game average; 5,040 assists (6.1 per game); 4,830 rebounds (5.9 per game); 681 steals; a .490 field goal percentage; and a .789 free throw percentage.

Frazier averaged 20 or more points per season six times, and his top scoring season came in 1972 with 1,788 points, a 23.2 average. He dished out 600 or more assists two times; 500 or more four times; and 400 or more eight times. Posting better per-game averages in the playoffs than the regular season, he scored 1,927 points (20.7 average); dealt 599 assists (6.4) and grabbed 666 boards (7.2) in 93 post-season games.

After 10 years with the Knicks and parts of three seasons with the Cleveland Cavaliers, Frazier retired in 1979. He was inducted into the Atlanta Sports Hall of Fame in 2009.

101 ATLANTA
SPORTS LEGENDS

"The best rebounding guard I've ever seen ... perhaps the best all-around guard in the history of the game."

— NBA great Jerry Lucas

BY THE NUMBERS

COLLEGIATE CAREER

- The Sporting News All-America second team (1967)
- Division II All-America (1964, 1965)
- Averaged 17.7 ppg in 50 games
- Led SIU to 1965 NCAA Division II Tournament, lost in finals to Evansville, 85-82 in overtime
- Named to All-Tournament Team
- Named Division I All-America (1967)
- Led SIU to 1967 NIT over Marquette, 71-56
- Named MVP of 1967 NIT

PRO CAREER

- NBA New York Knicks (1967-77)
- NBA Cleveland Cavaliers (1977-80)
- NBA All-Rookie Team (1968)
- All NBA First Team (1970, 1972, 1974, 1975)
- All-NBA Second Team (1971, 1973)
- NBA All-Defensive First Team (1969, 1970, 1971-75)
- Seven-time NBA All-Star (1970-76)
- NBA All-Star Game MVP (1975)
- NBA championships with the New York Knicks (1970, 1973)
- In 825 NBA games, averaged 18.9 points per game
- In 93 playoff games, averaged 20.7 points per game
- Still remains New York Knicks all-time assist leader (4,791)
- Knicks retired his No. 10 jersey (Dec. 15, 1979)
- NBA 50th Anniversary All-Time Team (1996)

NOMAR GARCIAPARRA

One of the best shortstops in baseball, Garciaparra was the Boston Red Sox's first round draft pick in 1994, straight out of Georgia Tech. It wasn't long before Garciaparra began making the same impact in the pros that he did in college, becoming only the sixth unanimous selection in Major League history for Rookie of the Year in 1996. The next year, he established himself as one of the game's best infielders, making spectacular plays in the field and hitting .306 with 30 homers.

While in the American League, Garciaparra became a five-time All Star (1997, 1999, 2000, 2002 and 2003). In 1999 and 2000, he was the AL batting champion, (hitting .357 and .372, respectively) and had 21 career hitting streaks of 10 or more games and four streaks spanning at least 20 games, including a career-best 30-game streak.

Garciaparra, often compared with two of his contemporaries, New York Yankees infielders Alex Rodriguez and Derek Jeter, also was known for his idiosyncratic tics when batting, including an elaborate routine of glove adjustments before each pitch. He began the 2004 season on Boston's disabled list with an Achilles tendon problem. After a contract dispute, he was dealt to the Chicago Cubs in the National League before the end of the season. The Achilles and a nagging groin injury were issues down the stretch for Garciaparra, who also suffered a wrist injury after joining the Cubs.

Despite the injuries, Garciaparra continued to hit the ball hard after changing leagues. However, he was lacking his usual home-run power. An aggressive hitter like most of the Cubs, he swung at the first pitch nearly 50 percent of the time. The high grass and tough winds at Wrigley Field held down Garciaparra's batting average there. He finished his injury-shortened 2005 season batting .283.

In 2006, he returned to the Dodgers, moving to first base, and after receiving more than six million votes, made his sixth All-Star Game appearance; he also was awarded the National League Comeback Player of the Year in 2006. He played third base in 2007, but was hit by a pitch during Spring Training '08, leading to one of two DL appearances that season. He became a free agent after the '08 campaign and signed with the Oakland Athletics for 2009.

Garciaparra, himself an expert soccer player, also made headlines off the field when he married Mia Hamm, a two-time Olympic gold medal winner in women's soccer. In 2000, he established the Nomar 5 Foundation, which supports community organizations that work for the well-being of children.

BY THE NUMBERS

TEAMS
Boston Red Sox (1996-2004)
Chicago Cubs (2004-2005)
Los Angeles Dodgers (2006-2008)
Oakland Athletics (2009)

CAREER HIGHLIGHTS AND AWARDS
2x consecutive AL Batting Titles (1999 .357) (2000 .372)
6x All-Star selection (1997, 1999, 2000, 2002, 2003, 2006)
Silver Slugger Award winner (1997)
1997 AL Rookie of the Year
2006 NL Comeback Player of the Year

FRANCES POOLE KING GARLINGTON

Taking up trapshooting so she could hunt with her husband and daughter, this Atlanta native held or tied 17 world trapshooting records.

In 1952, Garlington hit 200-of-200 targets in the 1952 Georgia State Trapshooting Championships, and also captured the prestigious North American Women's Clay Target and Dayton Homecoming championships in 1952. The 1952 captain of the Sports and Field Magazine 1952 All-American trapshooting team, she made this team 10 times during her career.

The future shotgun queen took up trapshooting in 1941 so she could hunt with her husband, Clyde King Jr., and their daughter in the field. That year, she shot her first registered targets; her first major victory came at the 1946 Grand when she and her husband won the Husband-and-Wife championship, and she placed third in the Champion of Champions race.

The following year Garlington was runner-up in the Georgia State 16-yard championship and several months later won the women's Grand American Handicap. In 1948 she won the Southern Zone open handicap; in 1949, she finished the season fourth in the nation.

Three times named Female Athlete of the Year by *The Atlanta Journal Constitution*, Garlington won the Georgia 16-yard championship in 1950, averaging 95 percent that year on 5,650 targets, third rating among women shooters. She again won the Georgia State championship in 1951 and 1952 (that same year she defeated her husband in a shootoff for the all-around, and he bested her in a tiebreaker for the handicap.)

In 1957 Garlington again won the women's Grand American Handicap. After tying for the Champion of Champions race six times, she finally won the crown at her last Grand in 1962.

Garlington fired her last registered targets in 1963, winning the Peach State women's championship for the 20th time. During her 23 years at the traps she shot 62,150 16-yard targets and approximately the same number of doubles, handicap and practice. As a result of her shooting abilities, Frances was inducted in the Trapshooting Hall of Fame, sharing this honor with only two other women, including Annie Oakley.

BERNIE "BOOM BOOM" GEOFFRION

To an Atlantan in the early 1970s, the game of ice hockey might as well have been invented on another planet. But the NHL awarded a franchise to Atlanta on Nov. 9, 1971, and almost six months later, the newly christened Atlanta Flames made Bernie "Boom Boom" Geoffrion became the franchise's first head coach.

During a time in which conservative league purists claimed Atlanta would make their beloved game a laughingstock, the ex-Montreal Canadien right winger and Hockey Hall of Famer led the Flames to the playoffs in only their second year. That record would stand for decades, until the NHL's vast expansion and resulting rule changes today allow almost three-fourths of its teams to qualify for post-season championship play.

"Boom Boom" gained NHL fame for his hard shot and feisty temperament. Born and raised in Montreal, he played right wing for the Montreal Canadiens' dynasties in the 1950s and '60s, and helped win the Stanley Cup an amazing six times during his time there. Many claim Geoffrion invented and perfected the slapshot, not bad for a kid who was once told by the assistant coach of a junior hockey team that he'd never make it in big-time hockey. From the moment he joined the NHL, he proved to be a talented and determined star. It was no surprise when the league named him Rookie of the Year in 1952.

Geoffrion broke his nose nine times and had 400 stitches during his 16-year NHL playing career. He also had numerous stomach problems and operations, but they never seemed to slow him down. During the 1960-61 season, he became only the second NHLer to net 50 goals in a season. He played in 11 NHL All-Star contests, and led postseason players in points with 18 (1956-57) and 12 (1959-60).

Geoffrion retired from the Canadiens in 1964. For a brief time he coached minor league hockey, hoping one day to coach his hometown club. He came back from his retirement in 1966 and played two more seasons with the New York Rangers, leading the team in scoring for the first few weeks of his first season back.

In 1972, NHL expansion came south of the Mason-Dixon Line, and "Boom Boom" was named head coach of the Flames. Geoffrion really took to Atlanta, even though he said it felt a little strange to have hockey in the deep South. He was a big hit with fans, and remained in Georgia over the summers.

Geoffrion coached the Flames for two and a half years and went on to become the team's vice president. In 1979 Geoffrion realized his dream of coaching the Canadiens, but only lasted 30 games due to stomach problems. As one of the most determined players in the history of the game, his place in hockey history was secure and he was inducted into the Hall of Fame in 1972.

The Canadiens announced on Oct. 15, 2005, that Geoffrion's uniform number 5 would be retired on March 11, 2006. On March 8, Geoffrion was diagnosed with stomach cancer after a surgical procedure uncovered it. Doctors attempted to remove the tumour, but found that the cancer had spread too far. Geoffrion died at the age of 75 in Atlanta on March 11, the day his jersey number was to be retired. His death also came exactly 10 years to the day that the Montreal Forum had closed its doors, in 1996.

 *"Boom Boom was an incredible man who meant a great deal to me, and I'm fortunate to have called him a friend and a mentor."*

— Bob Hartley, former Atlanta Thrashers coach

LET'S DON'T FORGET:

Jacques Richard. The very first amateur player picked for an Atlanta professional ice hockey team ... Drafted in 1972, Richard played three seasons for the Flames, his best season coming in 1973-74, with 27 goals, 16 assists, and 43 points ... Had an assist in first NHL game, which was also first game in Atlanta/Calgary franchise history ... Traded to the Buffalo Sabres in 1975.

Tom Lysiak, Eric Vail and Willi Plett. A trio of Flames whose line became the most famous in Atlanta hockey history, The Downtown Connector. Lysiak is the Atlanta Flames all-time career leader in points and goals, respectively. He recorded 155 goals, 276 assists, and 431 points, while Vail recorded 174 goals, 209 assists and 383 points.

TOM GLAVINE, GREG MADDUX AND JOHN SMOLTZ

This trio of pitching greats – all sure-fire first-ballot Hall of Famers – comprised Major League Baseball's best pitching rotation of the 1990s. The three pitchers guided the Atlanta Braves to the 1995, '96, and '99 National League flags. They also led the Braves to the club's sole World Series championship (1955). Among them, they won seven Cy Young Awards from 1991-98.

During the decade, Glavine was one of the National League's top pitchers, on his way to becoming a five-time 20-game winner; a two-time Cy Young Award winner; and one of only 23 pitchers to earn 300 career wins.

But Glavine's first years as a big-league pitcher weren't so stellar. He was 33–43 from 1987-90, including 17 losses in '88. But along with the Braves, his fortunes turned around in', when he won 20 games and posted a 2.55 ERA. This was the first of three consecutive seasons with 20 or more wins, and a year in which he won his first Cy Young. The '91 starting rotation had Glavine as the ace along with Steve Avery, Charlie Leibrandt, and another future NL Cy Young winner, Smoltz.

The Braves defeated the Cleveland Indians in 6 games in the 1995 World Series, and Glavine was named the Series MVP. He won games two and six, highlighted by eight innings of one-hit shutout baseball in game six. (The only run in that game was a solo 6th-inning home run by the Braves' David Justice.)

Glavine also went to four other World Series with the team (1991, 1992, 1996 and 1999). Glavine became the last major league pitcher—and the only pitcher active in 2007—to win 20 games in three consecutive years (1991–1993).

In 2003, Glavine signed as a free agent with the rival New York Mets, but his years in New York never matched the success he had in Atlanta, with the exception of 2006, when he finished with a 15-7 record and a 3.82 ERA. That was the same year in which Atlanta's remarkable run of consecutive division championships came to an end, when the Mets won the NL East title.

On Aug. 5, 2007, Glavine won his 300th game against the Chicago Cubs, becoming 23rd pitcher to win 300 games, and the fifth left-handed pitcher to do so.

Glavine declined a one-year, $13 million contract option for the 2008 season with the Mets, and returned to the Braves in 2008. But for the first time in his career, the left-hander went on the disabled list not once but twice, cutting short his 2008 campaign. After recovering from an off-season of surgery and rehabilitation, he was attempting to become the Braves' fifth starter for the 2009 season, but was released from the team before the 2009 All Star break.

Maddux joined Glavine and Smoltz in 1993. The Chicago Cubs drafted Maddux in the 1984 amateur draft's second round. He made his major league debut in September 1986 as the youngest player in the big leagues. In 1987, his first full season in the majors, Maddux posted a 6-14 record and 5.61 ERA, but he flourished in 1988, finishing 18-8 with a 3.18 ERA. This began a streak of 17 straight seasons in which Maddux recorded 15 or more wins, the longest such streak in history.

After consecutive 15+-win seasons in '89, '90 and '91, Maddux won 20 games in

1992, tied for the NL lead, and was voted his first National League Cy Young Award. Maddux signed a five year $28 million deal with Atlanta in time for the 1993 season.

Maddux was Major League Baseball's first pitcher to win the Cy Young Award for four consecutive years (1992-95), during which he had a 75-29 record with a 1.98 ERA, while allowing less than one runner per inning. He is also the only pitcher in history to win at least 15 games in 17 consecutive seasons.

Maddux returned to the Cubs as a free agent prior to the 2004 season, a campaign during which he won his 300th career victory. In 2005, he become the 13th member of the 3000 strikeout club and only the ninth pitcher with both 300 wins and 3,000 strikeouts. But his 13–15 record in 2005 was his first losing record since 1987, thus ending a string of 17 consecutive seasons with 15 or more wins.

Maddux was traded for the first time in his career to the Los Angeles Dodgers in 2006, then in the middle of a playoff race. On Dec. 5, 2006, Maddux agreed to a one-year, $10 million deal with the San Diego Padres. In 2007, Maddux reached 13 wins for the 20th consecutive season, passing Cy Young for that major league record.

Maddux was traded back to the Dodgers late in the 2008 campaign, during which time he won his 355th game, moving him into 8th place in all-time wins. Maddux ranks tenth in career strikeouts with 3,371, second to Randy Johnson among active pitchers. His strikeout total is balanced against 999 walks. For the 2008 season, he posted an 8–13 record. Maddux received his 18th Gold Glove Award in November 2008, extending his own major league record. He announced his retirement the following month.

Smoltz was born in Detroit and drafted by his hometown Tigers. In September 1987, Detroit traded him to the Braves for Doyle Alexander, in a deal that gave the Tigers the AL East title in the short term, and Atlanta a pitching ace for more than a decade.

Smoltz was a cornerstone of the Braves historic worst-to-first season in 1991, which led the team to the World Series. In game seven against the Minnesota Twins, he laid the groundwork for his reputation as one of the best postseason pitchers in baseball history. For seven innings, Smoltz shut out the Minnesota Twins before giving way to the bullpen, which lost the game in the bottom of the 10th. Smoltz fashioned a 1.29 ERA in 14 innings in that series, striking out 11 batters and issuing just one walk.

In 1992, Smoltz ran his career postseason record to 5-0 when he won two more games in the NLCS and game five of the World Series. He won the Cy Young Award in '96, when he was 24-8 with 276 K's for the pennant-winning Braves.

In 2002, recovering from an arm injury that had shelved him the previous season, he was moved to the bullpen to become the team's closer. He then set a National League record with 55 saves, just two shy of the major league record. Smoltz is the first pitcher to win the Cy Young Award as a starting pitcher, and later win the Rolaids Relief Man Award for leading the league in saves (1996 and 2002).

Smoltz returned to the Braves starting lineup in 2005 season, where he was once again the cornerstone of the lineup. He pitched the team's only postseason victory against the Houston Astros that year, once again solidifying his stellar postseason record. He became the 16th member of the 3,000 strikeout club on April 22, 2008 when he fanned Felipe Lopez of the Washington Nationals in the third inning at Turner Field in Atlanta. But like Glavine, Smoltz spent a great deal of the '08 season on the DL.

In January 2009, Smoltz signed a contract with the Boston Red Sox, with the anticipation he would be able to join the club in mid-season after attempting to comeback from his latest surgery. He made his debut with the Red Sox before the 2009 All-Star break, but was released shortly therafter. He then signed with the St. Louis Cardinals and made his debut with them on Aug. 23, 2009.

BY THE NUMBERS
TOM GLAVINE

Career statistics (through 2008)
- Win–Loss 305–203
- Earned run average 3.54
- Strikeouts 2,607

TEAMS
- Atlanta Braves (1987–2002)
- New York Mets (2003–2007)
- Atlanta Braves (2008)

Career highlights and awards
- 2x Cy Young Award winner (1991, 1998)
- 10x All-Star selection (1991, 1992, 1993, 1996, 1997, 1998, 2000, 2002, 2004, 2006)
- World Series champion in 1995
- Led NL in wins in 1991, 1992, 1993, 1998, and 2000

BY THE NUMBERS
GREG MADDUX

Career statistics
- Win–Loss record 355–227
- Earned run average 3.16
- Strikeouts 3,371

Teams
- Chicago Cubs (1986–1992)
- Atlanta Braves (1993–2003)
- Chicago Cubs (2004–2006)
- Los Angeles Dodgers (2006)
- San Diego Padres (2007–2008)
- Los Angeles Dodgers (2008)

Career highlights and awards
- 8x All-Star selection (1988, 1992, 1994, 1995, 1996, 1997, 1998, 2000)
- World Series champion (1995)
- 18x Gold Glove Award winner (1990, 1991, 1992, 1993, 1994, 1995, 1996, 1997, 1998, 1999, 2000, 2001, 2002, 2004, 2005, 2006, 2007, 2008)
- 4x NL Cy Young Award winner (1992, 1993, 1994, 1995)
- 4x NL TSN Pitcher of the Year (1992, 1993, 1994, 1995)

BY THE NUMBERS
JOHN SMOLTZ

(through 2008)
- Win-Loss 210-147
- Saves 154
- Earned run average 3.26
- Strikeouts 3,011

TEAMS
- Atlanta Braves (1988-2008)
- Boston Red Sox (2009)
- St. Louis Cardinals (2009)

Career highlights and awards
- Cy Young Award winner (1996)
- 8x All-Star selection (1989, 1992, 1993, 1996, 2002, 2003, 2005, 2007)
- World Series champion in 1995
- Led NL in wins in 1996 and 2006
- Led NL in saves in 2002
- Led NL in strikeouts in 1992 and 1996

LET'S DON'T FORGET:

Gene Garber. Relief pitcher for the Atlanta Braves who ended Pete Rose's 44-game hitting streak (a National League record) in 1978 ... Rose was chasing Joe DiMaggio's major league record 56-game hitting streak ... Career spanned 20 years (1969-1988) ... Among the all-time leaders in relief wins (96) and saves (218) ... 102-48 record over eight seasons in minor league and winter ball ... Combined with his nasty change up, Garber's signature corkscrew move on the mound baffled batters for almost two decades.

Leo Mazzone. Longtime pitching coach for the Atlanta Braves whose reputation for developing rookie pitchers and reviving the careers of veteran ones is unmatched in professional baseball ... Braves' pitching staff finished first or second in ERA from 1992 through 2002 ... Nine pitchers under Mazzone's tutelage have won 20 games or more ... Coached Atlanta's legendary trio of Glavine, Maddux and Smoltz in the 1990s ... After Maddux's and Glavine's departure, Mazzone tutored such pitchers as Russ Ortiz, Mike Hampton, Horacio Ramirez, Chris Hammond, John Burkett, Kevin Millwood, Kerry Ligtenberg, Jaret Wright, and countless others into winners ... One of the most recognizable coaches in baseball, tirelessly rocking back and forth on the dugout bench during games.

HENRY W. GRADY

The "Spokesman of the New South," *The Atlanta Constitution's* Grady was the region's very first baseball executive.

An avid sports fan, Grady was responsible for his paper's coverage of the rapidly-growing game of baseball in the 19th century. In fact, legend has it that while as managing editor of the *Constitution*, Grady personally covered the costs of the telegraph wire service that was used to transmit scores throughout the South to the paper.

On Nov. 23, 1884, the Southern League was formed in Montgomery, AL, with Grady as president. Grady took his duties seriously, so much so that some teams threatened to withdraw before the inaugural season was over. He was strict in his demands that players refrain from associating with "questionable characters." He wanted nothing to prevent baseball from becoming a wholesome, family-oriented entertainment medium, which would make the game all the more profitable.

The Southern League's inaugural season came in 1885, with Atlanta winning the league pennant, thus setting in motion a traditional of baseball excellence that continues to this day.

After graduating from the University of Georgia, Grady held a number of journalistic jobs with the *Rome Courier*, the *Atlanta Herald* and the *New York Herald*. He joined the *Atlanta Constitution* and, in 1880, bought a one-fourth interest in the paper. He quickly built the newspaper into the state's most influential with a national circulation of 120,000.

BRYAN MOREL "BITSY" GRANT

Nicknamed "Bitsy" because of his 5-foot, 4-inch frame, Grant is arguably the greatest tennis player Atlanta has ever produced.

Grant won the U.S. title three times (1930, '34 and '35). He also had many great moments on the grasses of Forest Hills, reaching the U.S. semis in 1935 by defeating second-seeded Don Budge, and in 1936, losing to eventual champion Fred Perry. He was a quarterfinalist in 1937, and reached the same round a year later.

Between 1930 and 1941 Grant was ranked nine times in the U.S Top 10, including No. 3 in 1935 and '36. In 1936 and '37 he was in the World Top 10, Nos. 8 and 6 respectively. A member of the United States' Davis Cup team from 1935-37, Grant reached the Wimbledon quarterfinals in 1936 and '37; and was the National Clay Court champion in 1930, '34 and '35. Grant also won eight of 11 tournaments in 1935.

Grant was the smallest American man to attain championship stature, and continued to compete as a senior, winning 19 U.S. singles titles on the four surfaces: Grass Court-45s (1956 and '57), 55s (1965, '66, '67 and '68); Indoor 55s (1966); Clay Court-45s (1959, '60, '61 and '63), 55s (1965, '66, '67, '68 and '69), 65s (1976 and '77); and Hard Court-65s (1976).

Elected to the International Tennis Hall of Fame in 1972, Grant once played without shoes at Wimbledon and was asked by the queen of England if he was the barefooted boy from Georgia. "Yes'm," he answered, and later explained that was Southern for "yes, your Majesty."

What They've Said: *"He was a shy man that had somewhat of a gruff exterior, but he was incredibly funny. But his real legacy was he was one of the great Georgia triumvirate: Bobby Jones, Ty Cobb and Bitsy Grant, the greatest Georgia athletes of their era."*

Peter Howell, president of the Bitsy Grant Tennis Association

LET'S DON'T FORGET:

Frank "Hop" Owens. Won the Southern Intercollegiate singles and doubles titles at Georgia Tech ... Three-time state singles and four-time state doubles champion ... Member of the Georgia Tech and Georgia Sports halls of fame.

EDWARD BARTON HAMM

The first representative from a Georgia school to win an Olympic gold medal, Edward Hamm took first place in the long jump in the 1928 Amsterdam Olympic Games.

Hamm set the world record in the long jump with a leap of 25' 11 1/8" in a track meet in Boston in 1928, prior to going to Amsterdam. The U.S. track team at those games would go on to win seven more gold medals.

Born on April 13, 1906, Hamm was a high school standout, winning the state long jump three straight years; the 220-yard dash three straight years; and the 100-yard dash twice. In 1924, he earned an invitation to the Olympic trials when he set a high school world record of 24 feet, 2 5/8 inches. But he failed to qualify for the 1924 games, and was forced to wait until 1928.

In the meantime, Hamm entered Georgia Tech, where he continued to set both conference and national records. While at Tech, he captured the NCAA long jump and national AAU titles. By the 1928 Olympic Trials, Hamm was in his prime, setting a-then world record in the long jump at the trials.

On July 31, 1928, Hamm engraved his name into Olympic history. Fouling on his first two attempts, he then jumped 25 feet, 4 inches, setting a then-Olympic record and collecting the gold.

Hamm is a member of the Georgia Tech and Georgia Sports halls of fame. There are more than two dozen medals and plaques won by Hamm on display on Georgia Tech's campus.

LET'S DON'T FORGET:

George Griffin. Georgia Tech's head track and field coach from 1924-1942 and cross country coach from 1923-1974 ... Coached 1928 Olympic long jump gold medalist and two-time NCAA long jump champion Ed Hamm ... Cross country teams captured SEC Championships in 1935-1940 and 1942 ... Coached SEC individual cross country champions from 1935-1939 ... Selected as the 1972 Georgia coach of the year ... Also coached the Georgia Tech tennis program from 1923-1924, winning 22 of 23 matches ... Co-founder and member of the Georgia Tech Hall of Fame.

TOM HAMMONDS

An outstanding college player at Georgia Tech, Hammonds' jersey was retired after a career in which he became the No. 4 scorer in school history.

In the pros, Hammonds spent 12 seasons in the NBA and appeared in 21 post-season playoff games.

Hammonds was drafted by the Washington Bullets (now the Wizards) in 1989. During his rookie season, he appeared in 70 games and averaged 5.2 points per game and 2.9 rebounds per game. On Jan. 29, 1992, Hammonds scored a career-high 31 points against the New York Knicks. Hammonds was traded to the Charlotte Hornets during the 1991-92 season, but missed all 30 games following the trade due to a groin pull.

The 1993-94 season saw Hammonds begin the year in Charlotte and end in Denver with the Nuggets after he was waived in mid-season. Hammonds collected a career-high 17 rebounds against his old team that year, and provided the league's youngest team with much-needed bench strength and leadership. Denver made an surprising postseason run by shocking the top-seeded Seattle SuperSonics in the first round and then taking the Utah Jazz to seven games in the Western Conference semifinals. The Nuggets' opening-round win marked the first time in NBA history that an eighth-seeded team defeated a top-seeded team in the playoffs.

The following year saw Hammonds appear in 70 games, starting four times, playing a season-high 31 minutes and responding with season highs of 26 points and 12 rebounds against the Boston Celtics on Feb. 18. Hammonds scored in double figures 10 times, eight of them after the All-Star break.

In 1996-97, Hammonds notched his 3,000th career point; rebound No. 2,000 rebound came the following year.

Hammonds signed with the Minnesota Timberwolves in 1998, and enjoyed a seven-game stretch in early April when he averaged 14.9 points per game, including a season-high 23 points April 3 against the Sacramento King, his high in a Wolves uniform. On May 4 vs. the Houston Rockets, he went over the 10,000-minute plateau for his career.

Injuries then began sidelining Hammonds for extensive periods of time, and his final season in the NBA, for the Wolves, saw Hammonds miss 72 games.

Since retiring from basketball, Hammonds was involved in the drag racing scene, owning his own National Hot Rod Racing Association team, and he currently owns a car dealership in South Carolina.

LEE HANEY

One of the greatest bodybuilders in history, Haney is the only eight-time Mr. Olympia, surpassing the legendary Arnold Schwarzenegger's record of seven titles in bodybuilding's most prestigious event.

Haney, from the south Atlanta community of Fairburn, retired from his sport in 1991 after collecting his eighth Mr. Olympia, at the age of 32. He then became an educator and trainer, working with many world-class athletes, and also serving as a member of the President's Council on Physical Fitness and Sports.

Haney's contributions to his sport and to the notion of overall fitness have been recognized by the President's Council on Physical Fitness, the United States Sports Academy and the International Federation of Bodybuilding. Haney also established Harvest House, a non-profit retreat facility for children on a 40-acre farm near Atlanta which featured nature tours, a petting zoo, and an eight-week summer camp for 12-15 year olds. Haney received a degree in youth counseling from Spartanburg Methodist College.

Within the sports and fitness arena, Haney is revered among his peers for his comprehensive personal training techniques as well as his contributions to the integrity of exercise in general. Professional athletes and coaches looked to Haney for goal-specific sports training and nutrition programs during the off-season and for injury rehabilitation. Fellow Atlanta Sports Legend Evander Holyfield sought out Haney to run his training programs before fighting in two heavyweight title defenses. Haney also trained Philadelphia 76er Shawn Bradley in order to strengthen and build up the hoopster's post-injury, as well as turning baseball superstar Gary Sheffield from a shortstop into a powerful right fielder.

Haney also opened two fitness centers in Atlanta which provided supervised weight training, aerobic, and strength conditioning equipment in addition to extensive nutritional counseling. His first facility, The Lee Haney World Class Fitness Center is unique in that it was the official wellness center for the city of Atlanta.

BY THE NUMBERS

1979 Teen Mr. America - AAU, Overall Winner
1979 Teen Mr. America - AAU, Tall, 1st
1982 Junior Nationals - NPC, Overall Winner
1982 Junior Nationals - NPC, Heavyweight, 1st
1982 Nationals - NPC, Overall Winner
1982 Nationals - NPC, Heavyweight, 1st
1982 North American Championships - IFBB, Heavyweight, 1st
1983 Grand Prix England - IFBB, 2nd
1983 Grand Prix Las Vegas - IFBB, Winner
1983 Grand Prix Sweden - IFBB, 2nd
1983 Grand Prix Switzerland - IFBB, 3rd
1983 Night of Champions - IFBB, Winner
1983 Olympia - IFBB, 3rd
1983 World Pro Championships - IFBB, 3rd
1984 Olympia - IFBB, Winner
1985 Olympia - IFBB, Winner
1986 Olympia - IFBB, Winner
1987 Grand Prix Germany (2) - IFBB, Winner
1987 Olympia - IFBB, Winner
1988 Olympia - IFBB, Winner
1989 Olympia - IFBB, Winner
1990 Olympia - IFBB, Winner
1991 Olympia - IFBB, Winner

ANNE PARADISE HANSFORD

A trailblazer for women in the sport of basketball when professional opportunities did not exist, Hansford was the first woman from Georgia to become an all-American basketball player.

Born in Lincoln County, GA, Hansford was a three-time AAU All-American in 1947, 1948 and 1949. She earned that honor twice with the Atlanta Sports Arena Blues in 1947 and 1948 and with the Chatham Blanketeers (Elkin, N.C.) in 1949. Hansford helped lead the Blues to the 1947 National Women's AAU basketball championship – the city's very first national women's amateur basketball title – during an undefeated 40-0 season.

Hansford scored two key baskets with the Blues trailing the Nashville Goldblumes 18-13 in the fourth quarter of the 1948 championship game and sent it into overtime. She scored 360 points over a 36-game schedule in helping the Blues back to the AAU National Championship Tournament in St. Joseph, MO. Her team finished as national runners-up losing only three games in 1948 and winning 75 of 78 during the 1947 and '48 seasons.

Hansford scored 37 points against the Lanett All-Stars and posted 48 against an All-Star team from Lindale, AL, as a member of the Chatham Blanketeers in 1949. She also earned All-American honors for the third straight year and led Chatham to a fourth place finish in the national championship tournament.

Earlier in her career, Hansford played for the Walco All-Girls team from Atlanta in 1943 and '44, earning honorable mention All-American honors at the 1943 national tournament. The following year, she scored 72 points in Walco's three 1944 state tournament games.

Her prep career provided an indication of Hansford's remarkable collegiate career, when, while attending Mesan Academy in Lexington, GA, she became an All-American by leading Lexington's Mesan Academy to four consecutive undefeated seasons.

What They've Said: *"The first day of practice, I saw what I thought was the most talented girl basketball player I had ever seen. She was quick, fast, could jump about three feet from the floor up and had full court vision, big soft hands, a most unselfish player, excellent team player, positive attitude, respect for all players and coaches."*

— Thomas H. Riden, basketball coach at Mesan Academy, 1940-41

REV. JOHN H. & BILLIE HARDEN

The Hardens were owners of the Atlanta Black Crackers of the Negro Southern and Negro American leagues, and are often credited with keeping black baseball alive in Atlanta often in the face of overwhelming financial odds.

The Hardens owned Harden's Service Station on Auburn Avenue, and in 1937, purchased an interest in the Atlanta Black Crackers. The team's owner at the time, W.B. Baker, didn't have a bus to transport players from one game to another. After Baker sold the team outright to the Hardens one year later, the couple was faced with the proposition of learning how to run a baseball team from the ground up.

The Hardens invested a great deal of time and money into Black Crackers. Players recalled later that the couple bought the team major-league quality uniforms and equipment. Harden was the team's business manager, while Mrs. Harden served as team secretary. Their players always had money in their pocket for food and other expenses, and if the team was on the road for an extended barnstorming tour, Harden himself would wire money to his wife, who often traveled with the team.

Mrs. Harden's presence on the road not only encouraged her players to be on their best behavior, it also kept other owners from cheating the Black Crackers out of their proper share of gate receipts. Like her husband, Mrs. Harden had a keen sense of business and record keeping, and the Black Crackers were rarely shorted their just financial due on the road.

Nonetheless, life on the road was hard for the team. Besides the overwhelming nature of the segregated South, the Black Crackers' bus often broke down. Mrs. Harden recalled years later that the couple's biggest challenge was just keeping the team bus in working order.

The Hardens also negotiated with Atlanta Sports Legend Earl Mann, owner of the Atlanta Crackers, for the use of Ponce de Leon Ballpark, the white team's home facility. The Black Crackers used the park whenever their white counterparts were on the road.

Skilled in the art of public relations, the Hardens encouraged their players to visit local radio stations and newspapers, to help promote their games. They also worked with both white and black youth groups and community organizations.

When Jackie Robinson's shattered the baseball color line in 1947, it spelled the eventual end for the Atlanta Black Crackers and other all-black teams. The Hardens operated the team for a short while thereafter, but eventually folded the operation, as the nation's black ballplayers moved into the mainstream of the great American pastime.

 *"Everybody was so excited over the Negroes getting a chance to go into the majors. It was beautiful. Everybody was so happy. And as Jackie went in there would be others going in. Of course, this was giving them a chance to do what they hadn't been able to do, and we were happy for it."*
— Billie Harden

LET'S DON'T FORGET:

Norman Lumpkin. One of the fastest Atlanta Black Crackers of all time ... Nicknamed "Geronimo" by his teammates ... An outfielder who played from 1939 to 1948 for the Black Crackers, as well as other sandlot, semi-pro and Negro teams, including the first team to call themselves the Atlanta Braves ... Played all three outfield positions ... Consistently batted .300 or higher during his career.

James "Red" Moore. "The Prince of First Basemen" ... One of the most popular Atlanta Black Crackers of all time ... Joined the team in 1935 and rejoined them in time for their historic 1938 season ... On July 31, 1938, fans gave him a special day at the ballpark, presenting him with a new baseball mitt, dress shoes, a radio, food, ball caps, clothes and some small cash donations. "I was one well-dressed cat," he recalled.

MATT HARPRING

A four-year starter at Georgia Tech and the second three-time All-Atlantic Coast Conference First Team player in school history, Harpring was drafted in the first round by the Orlando Magic in 1998, the 15th overall selection.

Harpring finished his collegiate career at Georgia Tech ranked second on the Yellow Jackets all-time scoring list (2,225 points) and second all-time in rebounds (997) as well as being the school's all-time leader in free throws made (508) and attempted (675).

Harpring was named All-ACC three consecutive seasons (1995-96 to 1997-98). He averaged 17.9 points and 8.0 rebounds in 124 games. A GTE Academic All-America selection, Harpring is one of only 10 players in ACC history to surpass 2,000 points and 900 rebounds and had his No. 15 jersey prior to his final regular-season home game. As a senior, he averaged career-highs of 21.6 points per game and 9.4 rebounds per game as a senior, when he was named Third Team All-America. He also ranked second in the ACC in scoring and rebounding and 14th in NCAA Division I in scoring.

In the pros, Harpring was a 1998-99 NBA All-Rookie First Team selection after averaging 8.2 points per game and 4.3 rebounds per game in all 50 contests. Harpring was traded by the Magic to the Cleveland Cavaliers in 2000, and then was shipped to the Philadelphia 76ers in 2001.

After signing as a free agent with the Utah Jazz in 2002, Harpring finished first in voting for the Victor Award as the most improved player in the NBA He averaged career highs in points (17.6 points per game) and rebounds (6.5 rebounds per game) in 2002-03. He also tallied then back-to-back career highs with 30 points against the Los Angeles Clippers on 11/26/02 and 33 points against the Minnesota Timberwolves on 11/29/02. For the year, Harpring averaged over 32 minutes per game and dished 133 assists, both career highs.

BY THE NUMBERS

- College - Georgia Tech Draft 15th overall, 1998
- Pro career 1998–present

Teams

- Orlando Magic (1998–2000)
- Cleveland Cavaliers (2000–2001)
- Philadelphia 76ers (2001–2002)
- Utah Jazz (2002-present)

Awards

- 1999 NBA All-Rookie Team

BURWELL TOWNS (B.T.) HARVEY

A legendary figure in the Southern Intercollegiate Athletic Conference (SIAC), Harvey not only was the most successful athletics coach in Morehouse College history, but also one of the Southeast's.

A graduate of Colgate University, Harvey arrived at Morehouse in 1916 to teach physics and chemistry; he would remain at the college for 42 years. Harvey coached Maroon Tiger teams in football, basketball, and baseball, for 13 years, from 1916-29. In that time, Harvey's gridiron squads won 59 games, lost 24, and tied six times. His football teams won three conference championships, and were undefeated and untied on two occasions.

Under Harvey's guidance, Maroon Tiger basketball teams won 131 games, including 10 consecutive SIAC championships, and lost only 17 times. On the baseball diamond, Harvey's teams won 112 games, lost 45 and tied three contests. His Maroon Tigers captured four conference titles and tied for two others. Harvey was also the SIAC's first commissioner.

In 1969, Harvey was inducted into the Hall of Fame of the National Association of Directors of Athletics. He also is enshrined in the SIAC and Atlanta University Center Halls of Fame. The Morehouse football stadium was renamed in his honor in 1983.

ERNIE HARWELL

Besides a Hall of Fame broadcasting career, this Georgia native has the distinction of being the only announcer in baseball history to be traded for an actual player!

Harwell was the voice of the Atlanta Crackers from 1943, 1946-48, when the team arranged a trade with the Brooklyn Dodgers. The Dodgers needed an announcer when the legendary Red Barber was hospitalized with a bleeding ulcer, and the Crackers needed a catcher. Harwell was traded to the Dodgers for a catcher named Cliff Dapper. Harwell's only objection to the trade? Dapper was a minor leaguer (he was on the roster of the then-Montreal Royals, the Dodgers Triple A franchise).

Harwell broadcast for the Dodgers through 1949, and the New York Giants from 1950-53, where he made the call of Bobby Thomson's "shot heard 'round the world" in the 1951 National League pennant playoff game on NBC television. He broadcast for the Baltimore Orioles from 1954-59, and joined the Detroit Tigers in 1960, where he remained for more than 30 years.

Harwell retired in September 2002.

Harwell grew up in Atlanta, and worked as a paperboy for the *Atlanta Georgian*. He was an avid baseball fan from an early age, and was a batboy for the Atlanta Crackers. Since the age of five, he never had to buy a ticket for a baseball game. After graduating from Emory University, he began his career as a copy editor and sportswriter for the *Atlanta Constitution* and as a regional correspondent for *The Sporting News*. In 1943, he began announcing Cracker games on WSB radio.

What They've Said:

"Bobby Thomson... up there swingin'... He's had two out of three, a single and a double, and Billy Cox is playing him right on the third-base line... One out, last of the ninth... Branca pitches... Bobby Thomson takes a strike called on the inside corner... Bobby hitting at .292... He's had a single and a double and he drove in the Giants' first run with a long fly to center... Brooklyn leads it 4-2...Hartung down the line at third not taking any chances... Lockman with not too big of a lead at second, but he'll be runnin' like the wind if Thomson hits one... Branca throws... There's a long drive... it's gonna be, I believe... THE GIANTS WIN THE PENNANT!! THE GIANTS WIN THE PENNANT! THE GIANTS WIN THE PENNANT! THE GIANTS WIN THE PENNANT! Bobby Thomson hits into the lower deck of the left-field stands! The Giants win the pennant and they're goin' crazy, they're goin' crazy! I don't believe it! I don't believe it! I do not believe it! Bobby Thomson... hit a line drive... into the lower deck... of the left-field stands... and this blame place is goin' crazy! The Giants! Horace Stoneham has got a winner! The Giants won it... by a score of 5 to 4... and they're pickin' Bobby Thomson up... and carryin' him off the field!"

— Ernie Harwell, calling Bobby Thomson's 'Shot Heard 'Round the World'

JOHN HEISMAN

The man for whom the award for the nation's best college football player is named has a long and storied tenure with Atlanta and one of its premier universities, Georgia Tech.

A native of Cleveland, Ohio, Heisman was Tech's head football coach from 1904-19, compiling a 102-29-7 mark and leading Tech to the 1917 national championship. Four of his squads were undefeated: 1905, 1915, 1916 and 1917. And while Heisman also coached at Oberlin, Akron, Auburn, Clemson, Penn, Washington & Jefferson and Rice (his overall coaching record is 186-69-17), it was at Georgia Tech that he served the longest, turning the program into a national powerhouse.

Heisman played football in high school (the field on which he played is still used by the Titusville High School Rockets.) He then attended Brown University from 1887-89, and later transferred to the University of Pennsylvania from 1890-91. He played football as a lineman (tackle) and center at both Brown and Pennsylvania. After receiving a law degree he returned to college football as Oberlin College's first head football coach in 1892. Heisman's team won all seven of its games, including a victory over Michigan and two over Ohio State.

From there, Heisman coached at Akron University (5-2-0) in 1893; returned to Oberlin in 1894 (4-3-1); and took over at Auburn University for five seasons, winning 12 games, losing four, and tying two. In 1900, Heisman became coach at Clemson. His first team won all six of its games and he had a 19-3-2 record there in four seasons before moving on to Georgia Tech, where he had the longest stay of his 36-year career.

Heisman turned Georgia Tech into a football power. His 1915, '16, and '17 teams were all unbeaten, contributing to a 32-game undefeated streak, including two ties. Tech outscored its opponents 1,592 to 62 over that stretch. Its 222-0 victory over Cumberland in 1916 is the highest score ever recorded.

In 1920, Heisman returned to the University of Pennsylvania as coach and had a 16-10-2 record in three seasons. After a 7-2-0 mark at Washington and Jefferson in 1923, he finished his coaching career with four seasons at Rice Institute, where he was 14-18-3.

One of the sport's chief innovators, Heisman developed one of the first shifts, which was named for him. He was probably the first coach to have both guards pull to lead an end run, a forerunner of the Green Bay Packer power sweep of the 1960s. And he may have been the first to have the center toss the ball back instead of rolling or kicking it, though others claimed that honor.

An early advocate of legalizing the forward pass, Heisman was a proponent of dividing a game into quarters instead of halves. He was a founder and twice president of the American Football Coaches Association.

(Continued on next page)

JOHN HEISMAN

Totally devoted to the game of football, Heisman was also an accomplished public speaker and a Shakespearean actor. His speeches were devoted mostly to football and his acting was part time because football occupied him fully.

After retiring from coaching, Heisman became athletic director of the Downtown Athletic Club in New York City. In 1935, the club began awarding a trophy to college football's outstanding player. After Heisman died in 1936, the award became known as the Heisman Memorial Trophy.

Heisman is a member of the Atlanta Sports Hall of Fame.

LET'S DON'T FORGET:

George Gardner. Born in Atlanta ... High school and SEC football official from 1925-1947 ... Co-founder of the Atlanta Touchdown Club ... Pioneer of the Georgia Football Officials Association ... Played football at Georgia Tech from 1921-1924, captaining the 1924 team ... Inducted into the National Football Foundation College Football Hall of Fame as a football official ... Also a member of the Georgia Tech Hall of Fame.

Joe Guyon. Born in White Earth Indian Reservation, MN ... 1966 inductee into the Pro Football Hall of Fame ...1918 football All-American at Georgia Tech ... Helped lead the 1927 N.Y. Giants to the Professional Football Championship.

L.W. "Chip" Robert, Jr. A Georgia native who earned 15 letters between 1905-1909 in football, baseball, cross country and track and field at Georgia Tech ... Quarterbacked John Heisman's 1908 football, baseball and cross country teams ... Helped lead Georgia Tech to four consecutive victories over arch-rival Georgia ... Received a pro contract offer as an outfielder by the Detroit Tigers but opted for a business career ... Known as one of the most influential people in Georgia Tech athletics history.

EVANDER HOLYFIELD

The only boxer to ever win a world heavyweight championship title four times, Holyfield captured the imagination of the boxing and sporting world on Nov. 9, 1996, when he knocked out Mike Tyson, at one time the most ferocious fighter of his generation.

The youngest of nine children, Holyfield, born Oct. 19, 1962 in Atmore, Alabama, moved to Atlanta several years later with his family. As a child, Holyfield had dreams of representing his new hometown on the football field as an Atlanta Falcon. At the Warren Memorial Boy's Club in southeast Atlanta, Holyfield started out on the 65-pound team as offensive fullback and middle linebacker on defense. He quickly distinguished himself on the field, but it was an 8-year-old's curiosity about a restricted area at the boy's club that led Holyfield to his athletic destiny: boxing.

After daily requests that were always turned down, Holyfield finally wore down Carter Morgan, convincing the coach to let him join the boxing team. Under Morgan's guidance, Holyfield never lost a match between the ages of eight and eleven and, throughout his years as an amateur, he compiled an impressive boxing resume with a 169-11 record.

In 1983 Holyfield represented the United States in the Pan-American Games in Venezuela, where he won a silver medal. He followed the Pan Am experience up in 1984 by winning the National Golden Gloves Championship – with all of the wins by KO – and earned a spot on the U.S. Olympic Team. Holyfield was favored to win the light-heavyweight championship at the 1984 Los Angeles games, but instead received a bronze medal after a controversial end in the semifinals.

Soon afterward, Holyfield made his professional debut, winning four bouts in the junior heavyweight division before moving up to cruiserweight. He won his first world title in 1986 against the WBA's world cruiserweight champion, Dwight Qwai.

On Oct. 25, 1990, Holyfield fulfilled his lifelong dream of becoming the heavyweight champion of the world when he dropped James "Buster" Douglas – then the IBF, WBC and WBA champion – in three rounds. Holyfield was the first cruiserweight champion to win the heavyweight title.

Holyfield was ready to fight Tyson, and a fight was scheduled for Nov. 8, 1991, the most anticipated match of the season. The reigning champ began an intense training regimen for the title defense, but on October 18, the bout was cancelled when Tyson injured his ribs. Shortly thereafter, Tyson was found guilty of rape, and sentenced to prison before ever fighting Holyfield.

(Continued on next page)

EVANDER HOLYFIELD

In 1992, Holyfield suffered his first defeat in 29 professional fights, losing a unanimous decision to Riddick Bowe. A year later, in one of his career's toughest fights, Holyfield reclaimed the title from Bowe, thus becoming the third fighter in history – along with Muhammad Ali and Floyd Patterson – to regain the title.

But in 1994, Holyfield lost his titles to Michael Moorer in a narrow 3-2 decision. After the fight, Holyfield was told that he was suffering from career-ending heart problems. Doctors recommended that he retire from the ring. He heeded their advice, even as he prayed for healing.

Months later, after medical officials confirmed Holyfield's heart had healed, boxing officials reinstated the former champ after another battery of tests. Convinced that his heart had been healed by God, Holyfield returned to the ring in 1995 to fight Ray Mercer, dropping the 1988 Olympic gold medalist in the eighth round.

The following year, Holyfield finally met Tyson, knocking him out in the 11th round. Holyfield's victory stunned the sporting world, as Tyson, even after several years in prison, was as vicious and unrelenting as ever. In their bizarre 1997 rematch, Tyson bit Holyfield on the ear in the second round. He lost a point, and almost immediately thereafter bit Holyfield on his other ear. Tyson was disqualified.

By 1999, WBC World Champion Lennox Lewis was ready to take on Holyfield. Their March match was declared a draw after 12 rounds. A rematch eight months later went to Lewis, with Holyfield losing unanimously.

When Lewis was stripped of the WBA belt in 2000 for failing to defend his title against a specified contender, the WBA declared the title vacant and ordered Ruiz and Holyfield to meet for the world title belt. In August of the same year, Holyfield won a 12-round unanimous decision and made history by becoming the first boxer in history to be the world heavyweight champion four times. Holyfield is a member of the Atlanta Sports Hall of Fame.

"I didn't raise a quitter."
— Annie Laura Holyfield, mother

LET'S DON'T FORGET:

Joe Corley. One of the nation's foremost martial arts entrepreneurs ... Earned his black belt at 19; opened his first studio at 20; won three U.S. titles in the next three years; and founded the Battle of Atlanta at age 23, an event that continues to be one of the largest open martial arts tournaments in the world ... Member of the Black Belt Hall of Fame ... Frequent consultant to Atlanta media on child and personal safety topics.

Keith Vitali. A former U.S. and world karate and kickboxing champion turned action film star ... One of the nation's leading authorities on child protection and safety ... Frequent guest on The Oprah Winfrey Show ... Member of the Black Belt Hall of Fame ... Successful author of numerous karate instructional books ... Appeared in numerous commercial feature films ... Owner and chief instructor of numerous martial arts schools.

LOU HUDSON

A 13-year NBA veteran, "Sweet Lou" spent 11 seasons with the Hawks franchise, nine of those in Atlanta. Today, his jersey is one of the few that have been retired by the franchise and hangs high above the court in Philips Arena.

The 6-5, 210-pound forward ended his NBA career with 17,940 points and averages of 20.2 points per game, and 4.4 rebounds per game. His 17,940 points are the 48th-highest in NBA history. Hudson played in six NBA All-Star Games and was selected to the second team All-NBA unit in 1970. He was named to the NBA All-Rookie team in 1967, and in his nine Atlanta seasons, he scored 14,004 points (23.2 per game); dished out 1,938 assists; and grabbed 2,970 rebounds.

Hudson's best NBA campaign came in the 1972-73 season when he scored a career-high 27.3 points, grabbed 6.2 rebounds and dished out 3.4 assists per game. He scored 1,500 or more points each season for the Atlanta Hawks from 1969-74, and averaged 20 or more points in seven NBA seasons, all with Atlanta.

Hudson's 57 points against the Chicago Bulls on Nov. 10, 1969, ties Dominique Wilkins and Bob Pettit for the most points scored in a game by a Hawks player. He made 25 field goals in that contest, a mark that remains a franchise record. And he averaged 21.3 points in nine playoff seasons with the Hawks and Los Angeles Lakers.

A native of Greensboro, NC, Hudson was named as the 26th greatest sports figure of the 20th Century in the state of North Carolina by *Sports Illustrated*, and also was chosen as the 13th-best shooter in NBA history by CBSSportsLine.com on its 14-Man All-Shooter Team in 2001.

Hudson was selected in the first round of the 1966 NBA Draft by the St. Louis Hawks with the fourth overall pick. He helped lead the United States to the gold medal and an 8-0 record at the 1965 World University Games in Budapest, Hungary, and finished that tournament as the team's leading scorer with an average of 17.3 per game. During his All-American collegiate career at the University of Minnesota, he averaged 20.4 points and 8.9 rebounds per game. Hudson was among the first three black basketball players to ever sign with that school, and the Minneapolis Star Tribune ranked him as Minnesota history's 36th most important sport figure.

(Continued on next page)

LOU HUDSON

In 2007, Hudson was inducted into the Atlanta Sports Hall of Fame. Induction ceremony Emcee Bill Hartman – himself one of Atlanta's most recognized sports broadcasters and reporters - referred to Hudson as "Super Lou," as the basketball legend, slowed by a 2005 stroke, insisted on walking to the podium to accept the honor.

BY THE NUMBERS

Atlanta Hawks records that mark all time best in franchise history –

- Third all time leading scorer (16,049 points)
- Third in minutes played (25,825)
- Field goals made (6,570) and attempted (13,501)
- Fourth best per game average (22.0)
- Fifth in games played (730)
- Free throws made (3,527) and attempted (3,659)

CLAUDE HUMPHREY

The all-time sack leader for the Atlanta Falcons, Humphrey was one of the NFL's most featured defensive ends for more than a decade.

1968's No. 1 draft pick came from one of the tiniest football programs in the nation (Tennessee A&I State), and Humphrey then played for some of the most wretched professional football teams in the nation. But he took advantage of every opportunity that came his way, earning Defensive Rookie of the Year honors in 1968 and then appearing in a total of six Pro Bowls, including five in a row.

Born Nov. 19, 1947 in Memphis, TN, Humphrey spent 10 years with the Falcons and three with the Philadelphia Eagles. He was an NFL All Pro four times (1971, '72, '73, '74); an All-NFC pick in 1970, '71 and '73; and remains tied with Jeff Van Note for representing the Falcons in six NFL Pro Bowls (1970-74, '77). During his 127-game career in Atlanta, he started in each and every one.

Still the Atlanta career sack record holder with 62.5 that accounted for 510 yards (also a club record), Humphrey produced five seasons with 10 or more sacks – 1973 (10); 1977 (10); 1971 (12); 1974 (12.5); and 1976 (15).

Humphrey was a particular nemesis to the Falcons' most bitter rival, the New Orleans Saints. During a 1971 contest, Humphrey brought down New Orleans quarterbacks a total of four times. He also ranks among Falcon career leaders in fumble recoveries with 11, and safeties with two.

In 2008, Humphrey was inducted into the Atlanta Sports Hall of Fame, as well as into the Atlanta Falcons' Ring of Honor.

(Continued on next page)

CLAUDE HUMPHREY

BY THE NUMBERS

Career stats
- Sacks - 126.5
- Games - 171
- Safeties - 2
- 6x Pro Bowl selection (1970, 1971, 1972, 1973, 1974, 1977)
- 8x All-Pro selection (1969, 1970, 1971, 1972, 1973, 1974, 1976, 1977)
- 1968 NFL Defensive Rookie of the Year

LET'S DON'T FORGET:

Rufus Guthrie. Born in Atlanta ... An All-American lineman for Georgia Tech in 1962 ... Also selected first-team All-SEC by the Associated Press and United Press International ... Played in the All-American Game and Senior Bowl in 1961 ... First round draft pick by the Los Angeles Rams and second round pick by the AFL's San Diego Chargers in 1963, eventually signing with the Chargers.

George Hamilton Brodnax III. Atlanta native who was named first-team All-American in 1948 by Colliers Magazine ... Four-year letterman and three-year starter at end from 1945-48 ... Helped lead the Yellow Jackets to an overall two-year record of 19-3 from 1946 (9-2) to 1947 (10-1) ... Drafted by the Detroit Lions and San Francisco 49ers ... Lettered in four sports at Atlanta Boys High and was a state champion discus thrower his senior year.

JOHN "WHACK" HYDER

The second-winningest basketball coach in Georgia Tech history, "Whack" Hyder guided Tech to a 292-271 mark from 1952-73, a stint that included three upsets over the legendary Adolph Rupp's No. 1-ranked Kentucky teams; the NCAA Sweet 16 in 1959-60; and runner up in the SEC three times (1960, 1963, 1964). His team's 23-9 mark in 1971 was the most successful basketball season in Tech history at that time.

Born July 10, 1912 in Lula, GA, Hyder was one of the best all-around athletes in Georgia Tech history, lettering in basketball, baseball, cross country and track. He also earned a freshman letter in football, the sport in which he received his Tech scholarship because there were no basketball scholarships in those days.

After graduating from Georgia Tech in 1937, Hyder signed a professional baseball contract and played three years in the New York Yankees farm system. After a stint in the U.S. Navy in World War II, he returned to Tech in 1946. He was hired as an assistant basketball coach by Director of Athletics William Alexander, the same man who had offered him a scholarship to Tech after watching him play basketball for Monroe A&M prep school. He served as assistant coach under Roy McArthur until he was elevated to head coach prior to the 1951-52 season.

Hyder's tenure was highlighted by Georgia Tech's first NCAA Tournament appearance in 1960 as well as two trips to the National Invitation Tournament. His most famous victory was on Jan. 8, 1955, when his Yellow Jackets defeated the Kentucky powerhouse, 59-58, to end the Wildcats' 129-game home winning streak. The record-setting 1971 campaign ended with a loss to the North Carolina Tar Heels in the NIT finals.

Hyder also coached Tech's first two all-America players in Roger Kaiser and Rich Yunkus and was twice named Southeastern Conference Coach of the Year.

What They've Said:

"Coach Hyder was a special person who loved Georgia Tech very much. I often heard his former players talk about how much they loved playing for Coach Hyder. He was a great friend and a great help to me during my coaching career."
— Bobby Cremins

"He was the best thing in the world for me. He had so much patience in dealing with his players, and you could tell how much he cared for each of us as individuals. Because of that, we respected him so much and wanted to play that much harder for him."
— Roger Kaiser

ERNIE JOHNSON SR.

Johnson's baseball playing career was over by the time the Milwaukee Braves relocated south of the Mason-Dixon line in 1966. But Johnson came with the team anyway – as a broadcaster - and he's been part of Atlanta's sports scene ever since.

The former Braves pitcher played nine seasons in the majors (eight with the Braves and one with the Baltimore Orioles. The Cleveland Indians picked him up after his stint in Baltimore, but released him before the 1960 season.) In Game Six of the 1957 World Series, Johnson pitched well but lost the contest when he surrendered a solo home run to the New York Yankees' Hank Bauer.

Johnson's smooth voice and knowledge of the game earned him his first television job as the host of a baseball show called "Play Ball!" on a local Milwaukee station. From there, he was hired as the color commentator on Braves radio in 1962. He relocated to Atlanta when the team moved south to begin the 1966 season.

For years, Johnson teamed with Milo Hamilton to become one of the South's most recognizable broadcast teams before cable TV and multimillion-watt radio stations. He was instrumental in helping another Atlanta Sports Legend, Pete Van Wieren, get his first job with the Atlanta Braves.

Another Atlanta Sports Legend, Skip Caray, had his own favorite story about Johnson: When turning the mike over at the end of an inning, Skip remarked, "And now, here's the Voice of the Braves, Ernie Johnson." Embarrassed by the title, Ernie replied during the next commercial, "Skip, don't call me the "Voice" of the Braves...we're all the voices of the Braves here."

In 2007, Johnson was inducted into the Atlanta Sports Hall of Fame. He was introduced by his son, Ernie Johnson, Jr., a respected and nationally known broadcaster in his own right.

BOBBY JONES

Without question, this Atlanta native is the greatest golfer to come from the Peach State and one of the truly greats of all-time.

Jones captured 13 national golf titles in a seven-year span: the U.S. Open (four); the U.S. Amateur (five); the British Open (three); and the British Amateur (one). Jones won the Grand Slam of golf in 1930 by taking the American and British Amateur and Open crowns.

Jones was born on St. Patrick's Day, March 17, 1902, as the only son of Colonel Robert P. Jones, a prominent Atlanta lawyer. He was such a sickly child that he was unable to eat solid food until he was five years old. When he was six, his family moved to a summer home near the East Lake Country Club where young Bobby grew stronger and began playing sports, particularly baseball and golf.

Jones' first golf club was a cut-down cleek, an early version of a one-iron, given to him by a neighbor. Jones never had any formal lessons, learning the golf swing by mimicking East Lake's Scottish professional, Stewart Maiden.

At age six, Jones won his first tournament against three other children at East Lake. At nine, he won the Atlanta Athletic Club junior title. When he was 13, he won an invitational tournament in Birmingham, Alabama. At 14, Jones won the East Lake Invitational and the Georgia Amateur, defeating his good friend Perry Adair. Adair's father already had made plans to take his son to the 1916 U.S. Amateur and with the Jones family's permission, he took Bobby along too, making him the youngest player ever to qualify for and play in a U.S. Amateur Championship. Jones stunned 1906 U.S. Amateur champion Eben Byers and Pennsylvania Amateur champion Frank Dyer before losing in the third round to defending champion Bob Gardner, making Jones an overnight sensation.

Jones continued to mature both personally and as a player, developing the character he would need to win his first championship, the 1923 U.S. Open.

From 1923-30, Jones dominated the game of golf, winning at least one national championship every year and 13 of the 21 major championships he entered. He was so completely dominant during that period that his two primary rivals - Walter Hagen and Gene Sarazen - never won any U.S. or British Open in which Jones played.

(Continued on next page)

BOBBY JONES

In 1926, Jones became the only amateur to win both the U.S. and British Opens in the same year, receiving a ticker tape parade down Broadway in New York City. In 1927, he returned to St. Andrews to defend his Open title and in the process erased the bitter disappointment he had suffered six years earlier. Declaring that the trophy would remain in St. Andrews if he should win, Jones endeared himself to the people of St. Andrews, forming a kindred spirit with the birthplace of golf's residents that would flourish for all time.

In 1930, Jones accomplished the unthinkable by winning the U.S. and British Open and Amateur Championships, all in the same year. This tremendous feat, later dubbed the Grand Slam, had never been accomplished before or since. Fourteen years later, the Associated Press would call Jones' accomplishment sports history's all-time achievement.

Most of those who followed the game of golf assumed Jones would turn professional and continue to win championships for years to come. Having already dominated both professionals and amateurs, there seemed to be no limit to the number of tournaments Jones would win. But, just over a month after winning the Grand Slam, Bobby Jones shocked the world by retiring from golf at age 28.

In retirement, Jones continued to demonstrate his wide range of talents and interests. Having already contributed immeasurably to the game as a player, he proved himself to be equally impressive as a teacher, writer and golf course designer. Jones also assisted A.G. Spalding & Co. in designing the first set of matched golf clubs.

Perhaps Jones' greatest legacy to the game of golf was his design of Augusta National. Still considered one of the finest golf courses in the world, Augusta opened in 1933 and is home to the Masters, one of the four major tournaments played today.

In 1948, Jones was diagnosed with syringomyelia, a rare and degenerative disease of the central nervous system. The author of one of golf's most graceful and powerful swings lived out his days crippled by the deadly disease, passing away on Dec. 18, 1971, at the age of 69.

Jones was part of the inaugural class of inductees into the Atlanta Sports Hall of Fame.

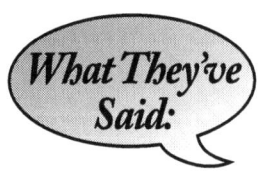

"Bobby Jones is not one in a million persons...I should say he is one in ten million-or perhaps one in fifty million."

— Legendary sportswriter Grantland Rice

CALVIN "MONK" JONES

With a lifetime record of 886-224, Jones' coaching career is made all the more remarkable by the fact that – for much of the time – his high school basketball teams had no facility in which to practice.

Born in Atlanta in 1925, Jones attended Booker T. Washington High School, and then went to Tuskegee University in Alabama. His first high school coaching job came in 1958, when he was named head girls' basketball coach for Booker T. Washington. His record in '58 was 14-8, followed by a 19-3 record the following year.

Jones moved to Atlanta's Carver High in 1962 as head coach of the boys' basketball team. In 1965, Carver won Atlanta's last black-only city championship, and followed up in 1966 by winning the state's first integrated Division AA basketball tournament.

While at Carver High, Jones' teams won three city, eight regional and two state championships. In 69, Carver fielded a team that averaged 115 points a game en route to a 31-1 record.

Jones became Georgia's first collegiate black basketball coach in 1975, when he was selected by Coach John Guthrie at the University of Georgia. While at UGA, Jones also served as a coach and recruiter for Vince Dooley's football program.

Jones received numerous awards and accolades throughout his career, beginning in 1966, when he was named high school coach of the year by the Atlanta Tip-Off Club. He also received numerous coach of the year awards from the Georgia Athletic Coaches Association, as well as distinguished service awards from the Atlanta Parks & Recreation Department for conducting basketball clinics throughout the city.

Jones was inducted into the 2009 class of the Atlanta Sports Hall of Fame.

"We had no gym back then, so every game we played was a road game, Coach Jones told us, 'Don't look back. Don't worry about what you didn't have; just create for the future.'"

— Roy Stanley, former player

ROSIE JONES

One of the most successful golfers in the history of the Ladies Professional Golf Association, this Atlanta resident won 13 LPGA tournaments from the time she joined the tour in 1982. She had four top-three finishes in 2002, and in 2003 won the Asahi Ryokuken International Championship at Mount Vintage, her 13th LPGA title.

Jones was a 1981 AIAW All-American in her fourth year of varsity golf at Ohio State University. Also in 1981, she was the third-lowest amateur at the U.S. Women's Open and a semifinalist at both the U.S. Women's Amateur and the Trans-National. Earlier in her amateur career, Jones won the New Mexico Junior Championship three consecutive years, 1974-76, and claimed the 1979 New Mexico State Championship title.

During her first season on the Tour (1982) Jones qualified by tying for seventh at the final qualifying tournament. Her best finish that year was a tie for 28th at the Mary Kay Classic. The following year, she finished fourth at the Peter Jackson Classic, and in 1984, Jones finished second twice, falling one shot shy of tying Hollis Stacy for the U.S. Women's Open title and then losing to Kathy Whitworth on the first hole of a sudden-death playoff at the Rochester International.

Jones' best finishes in 1985 was fifth at the Chrysler-Plymouth Classic, and in '86, seventh place at the du Maurier Classic. Her first LPGA Tour Victory came in 1987 with the Rail Charity Golf Classic, a year where she also notched the first hole-in-one of her career during the GNA/Glendale Federal Classic.

Jones captured the USX Golf Classic title in 1988, where she defeated LPGA Tour and World Golf Halls of Famer Kathy Whitworth in a sudden-death playoff. She also won the Nestle World Championship and Santa Barbara Open. In 1989, best finish was a tie for fourth at the Standard Register PING.

In 1990, Jones became the 20th player to eclipse the $1 million mark in career earnings, a year where her best finish was second place at the Mazda LPGA Championship. Her fifth career victory came in 1991 at the Rochester International. Jones' next victory didn't come until 1995 when she captured the Pinewild Women's Championship title by defeating Dottie (Pepper) Mochrie on the first hole of a sudden-death playoff. She recorded the third ace of her LPGA career during the first round of the Oldsmobile Classic.

Two titles came in 2001 - the Kathy Ireland Championship Honoring Harvey Penick after a playoff with Mi Hyun Kim, and the Sybase Big Apple Classic Presented by *Golf Magazine*. She crossed the $5 million mark in career earnings after her first win of the season; and recorded her career fifth hole-in-one during the second round of the McDonald's LPGA Championship Presented by AIG.

In 2002, Jones recorded four top-three finishes—second place at the LPGA Corning Classic and ties for third at the Kraft Nabisco Championship, Asahi Ryokuken International Championship at Mount Vintage and Safeway Classic; crossed the $6 million mark in career earnings after tying for 11th at the Evian

Masters; and qualified for her fifth Solheim Cup, posting a 2-1-0 record for the victorious U.S. Team.

In 2003, Jones 13th career LPGA title came at the Asahi Ryokuken International Championship at Mount Vintage, a year where she crossed the $7 million mark in career earnings at the Evian Masters.

BY THE NUMBERS
LPGA TOUR VICTORIES

2003: Asahi Ryokuken International Championship at Mount Vintage
2001: Kathy Ireland Championship, JAL Big Apple Classic
1998: Rochester International
1997: LPGA Corning Classic
1996: LPGA Corning Classic
1995: Pinewild Women's Championship
1991: Rochester International
1988: USX Golf Classic, Nestle World Championship, Santa Barbara Open
1987: Rail Charity Golf Classic

BY THE NUMBERS

- Career victories (last): 13 (2003)
- Career-low round: 62
- Career earnings (rank): $8,306,013 (6)
- LPGA career holes-in-one: 5
- Playoff record: 5-4
- International victories: 2

ROGER ALLEN KAISER

Kaiser is Georgia's only two-time basketball first-team All-American and the only basketball coach in state history to win not only one national collegiate championship, but four.

A native of Indiana, Kaiser scored 1,649 career points at Dale High School as a four-year varsity player. He was chosen as a member of the Indiana All-Star team in 1957. Named a first team All-American basketball in 1960 and 1961 for Georgia Tech, Kaiser scored 1,628 points in three varsity seasons. He also led the SEC in scoring in 1960 (22.8) and 1961 (23.8), and was a 1960 and 1961 All-SEC selection. In 1960 he led Tech to a 22-6 mark. At the time of his graduation in 1961, Kaiser held 18 of 25 Tech records involving field goals and free throws.

A two-sport star, Kaiser was a two-time captain and three-year Georgia Tech basketball and baseball letterman. He led Tech's baseball team in hitting and was named MVP in the SEC.

After college, Kaiser played two years of pro ball in the American Basketball League. In 1970, he entered the world of coaching, his first job being at West Georgia College. Four years later, his team won the first national collegiate crown ever won by a Georgia team. In 20 years at West Georgia, he turned out three All-Americans and six players who made it in the NBA.

Kaiser left West Georgia to start an athletics program at Life College, which was founded as a chiropractic school. Among the 15 national championships Life College sports teams won, three were Kaiser-coached basketball teams. In 10 years at Life, Kaiser produced 12 All-Americans. Eight times he was named conference Coach of The Year.

In 30 years of college coaching, Kaiser was named Coach of The Year in Georgia 11 times, state of Georgia Sports Hall of Fame Coach of The Year three times and NAIA Coach of The Year twice. And he was inducted into the Atlanta Sports Hall of Fame in 2009.

What They've Said:

"He was the best player I ever had, but that is only part of it. Everything he did, he did well. He had the drive for perfection, not just in sports but in the way he dressed. His shoes sparkled, front and back, and the belt buckle on his military uniform glistened."

— John "Whack" Hyder, Kaiser's basketball coach at Georgia Tech

KIM KING

One of the true legendary icons in Georgia Tech football history, King's relationship with the school began when he rewrote its record book as a quarterback.

King set 13 school records in three years including career yardage (2,763), completions (243) and attempts (460) and also a career mark for total yardage with 3,269. He was named *Sports Illustrated* Back-of-the-Week in 1966 when he passed for over 300 yards against Tennessee. He played in the Gator and Orange Bowls, and co-captained the 1967 team.

Prior to attending Tech, King was an All-City, All-State and All-American football player at Brown High, where he set Atlanta City School System records for most yards passing and total offense in 1961 and 1962. In 1963, he was the Atlanta Touchdown Club Back-of-the-Year, and MVP of the 1963 Georgia High School All-Star game.

King began his long association with Georgia Tech when he enrolled at the Institute in the fall of 1963. "The Young Lefthander" was a three-year starter at quarterback from 1965-67, leading the Jackets to berths in the Gator and Orange Bowls. One of his career's highlights came when he helped the Jackets to a victory over eighth-ranked Tennessee in 1966 and was named National Back of the Week by *Sports Illustrated*. He finished his career as Tech's all-time leading passer.

An outstanding student, King earned his bachelor's degree in Industrial Management from Tech in 1968, launching his highly successful business career. He founded Kim King Associates, Inc., one of Atlanta's foremost commercial real estate development firms, in 1972. His firm developed numerous projects and properties throughout Atlanta.

King remained an integral figure in Georgia Tech athletics throughout his life, and was highly instrumental in the program's growth. He chaired the initial feasibility study for what ultimately became the Arthur B. Edge Center, which houses Tech's athletics offices. In 1988, he was a driving force behind the agreement between the State Board of Regents and the Grant family heirs to add the name of Bobby Dodd to Tech's home field. He was active in fund-raising activities for cancer research as well as the Bobby Dodd Charities Foundation, Inc.

King also was admired by generations of Yellow Jacket fans for his role as color analyst on Tech's radio broadcasts. He joined the radio broadcast team in 1974 as the partner of Atlanta Sports Legend Al Ciraldo, and later worked with Wes Durham. Georgia Tech honored King by officially dedicating the Kim King Football Locker Room at Bobby Dodd Stadium/Grant Field.

King also served as president of the Atlanta Touchdown Club; the Georgia Tech Yellow Jacket Club; the Greater Atlanta Tech Club; and the Georgia Tech Letterman's Club. He served on the Scottish Rite Committee for the Georgia Tech-Georgia Benefit Game; the steering committee and board of directors of the Georgia Amateur Athletics Association; and was co-chairman of the Georgia Tech Success Center Project.

King died in 2004 after a battle with leukemia.

(Continued on next page)

KIM KING

What They've Said: *"Kim King is the true Tech Man, from the way he played on the football field to his successful business career, and most importantly, in the way he lived his life."*

— Georgia Tech head football coach Chan Gailey

LET'S DON'T FORGET:

Jim Breland. 1966 All-American center at Georgia Tech ... Selected first-team by American Football Coaches Association and Central Press ... Also became an Academic All-American ... Named the Atlanta Touchdown Club's Southeast Area Lineman of the Year ... Helped the Jackets to a 9-2 mark and a 1965 Orange Bowl berth against the Florida Gators ... Transferred to Tech from the United States Naval Academy ... Played on 7-3-1 Tech squad that upset 10th ranked Texas Tech 31-21 in the Cotton Bowl ... Drafted by the San Francisco 49ers in the 17th round of the 1966 NFL Draft.

Billy Lothridge. Second to Navy's Roger Staubach in the 1963 Heisman Trophy voting ... 1963 All-American ... 1962 and '63 All-SEC selection ... Placed eighth in the Heisman Trophy voting in 1962 ... Led Georgia Tech to a three-year mark of 21-10-1 including appearances in the Gator and Bluebonnet bowls ... Scored 33 career TDs (15 rush, 18 pass) ... Responsible for 204 points in three seasons (15 TDs, 51 PATs, 2FGs) ... Compiled 3,140 career yards of total offense (2,394 passing, 746 rushing) ... Had career punting average of 41.0 ... Set 16 school marks, 14 in 1963 alone ... Sixth round draft choice played professionally for nine years with Dallas, Los Angeles, Atlanta and Miami ... Member of the 1972 Miami Dolphins undefeated Super Bowl championship team ... Played with the Atlanta Falcons from 1966-71 averaging 41.3 yards per kick ... Led NFL in punting with a 43.7 and 443.3 average in 1967 and 1968 ... Tech football coach Bobby Dodd called him the most versatile quarterback he ever coached.

Billy Martin. One of Tech's greatest pass catching ends while teaming with high school teammate Billy Lothridge from 1961-1963 ... Earned All-American and All-SEC honors in 1963 ... Grabbed 56 career passes for 777 yards and six TDs ... Also earned SEC accolades in 1962 ... Drafted in the second round by the AFL's Kansas City Chiefs and NFL's Chicago Bears ... Played five years in the NFL with the Bears (1964-1965), Atlanta Falcons (1966-1967), and Minnesota Vikings (1968).

STEVE LUNDQUIST

One of the most successful swimmers in American competitive history, this Atlanta native (and member of the International Swimmers Hall of Fame) won two gold medals in the 100-meter breaststroke and 400-meter medley relay at the 1984 Los Angeles Olympic Games, with both gold-medal performances in then-world record time - 100-meter breaststroke (1:01.65) and 400-meter relay (3:39.40).

A member of the International Swimming Hall of Fame, Lundquist captured six gold medals at the 1979 and 1983 Pan Am Games. Also in 1983 he set a world record in the 100-meter breaststroke (1:02.28) and 400-meter medley relay (3:40.00). He also won two gold medals at the 1982 World Games.

Lundquist attended Woodward Academy and Jonesboro High School, where he was a three-time All-American. He then attended Southern Methodist University, where he was a four-time All-American and set nine individual collegiate records.

Lundquist was the first swimmer to break two minutes in the 200-yard breaststroke. He won every 100-yard breaststroke event he entered from 1980-1983. At 17 he broke his first world record and in his career he broke 15 world and American records. He first broke the 100-meter breaststroke world record in 1982 and held it until 1989 with the exception of one month (when John Moffet held it.) Lundquist also held the world record in the 200m IM in 1978. He set American records in the 100-meter and 200-meter breast and the 200-meter IM.

After the '84 Olympics, Lundquist spent much of his time volunteering his time for charitable organizations and making appearances on television and in movies. In 1996, when the Olympics were hosted in Atlanta, he was an Olympic torch bearer; the Clayton County master of ceremonies for the torch run; and also was the Olympic Flag Bearer at the 1996 Olympic Games.

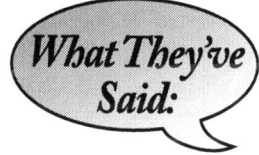

"We moved (to Lake Spivey) when he was very young. So, his backyard was the lake. He grew up with the water only being about 100 feet from our back door."
— Bob Lundquist, father

BY THE NUMBERS

- U.S. Honorary Olympic Team medalist, swimming, 1980
- United States Swimmer of the Year, 1982
- Olympia Award, 1983
- U.S. Olympic Team double gold medalist, swimming, 1984
- International Swimming Hall of Fame, inducted in 1990
- Georgia Sports Hall of Fame's youngest inductee, 1990
- Olympic flagbearer, torch-runner, emcee, 1996
- Voted America's Top Breast-Stroker of the Century, US Swimming
- Georgia State Games Cauldron Lighter, 1997
- 3rd place, Super Dogs Super Jocks, 1998

GEORGE BERNARD MALOOF

In 1958, St. Pius X Catholic High School opened in Atlanta and hired Maloof as its head football coach. Maloof kept going full speed for 26 years, posting a 168-85-12 won-lost record. His was the first Catholic school to win a state championship (1968). Along the way, he whipped his prep alma mater – The Marist School - and was twice named Georgia Class AA Coach of The Year.

Maloof was held in such high esteem that St. Pius named its football field after him and Marist dedicated a special game in his honor. It may be the only time a school honored a former coach of its arch-rival institution.

An Atlanta native, Maloof was a star student-athlete at Marist and Georgia Tech. In high school, he lettered four years in football, making All-State, All-Southern and prep All-American teams. He lettered four times in baseball, making the All-Greater Atlanta and All-State teams and picking up two more monograms for basketball. He played in the Georgia High School All-Star Game and was named the North Team's outstanding player in the game. The Atlanta Touchdown Club named him the most valuable prep lineman in Georgia.

In 1951, Maloof scored four touchdowns in leading Georgia Tech to a 48-6 rout of the Bulldogs, an unbeaten season (11-0-1) and the Southeastern Conference championship. No Jacket had ever put 24 points on the scoreboard against UGA. Maloof also played third base on Tech's baseball team and twice was named to the all-conference team.

When Maloof graduated from Tech in 1952, he went into the U.S. Air Force as a second lieutenant. He was picked to play on the Ft. Bragg All-Star football team and was chosen most valuable player in the 9th Air Force.

Coming back to Atlanta, Maloof joined Marist as assistant football coach. His stay was short-lived, as he moved to St. Pius only two years later.

Maloof had a chance to become an assistant college football coach at his alma mater in 1967 under head coach Bud Carson, but he turned down the offer.

Aside from his four-TD romp against the Bulldogs, Maloof's biggest thrill was Sept. 15, 1995, at halftime of the St. Pius-Chamblee game. A tent was placed in the Pius end zone and many of his former players and cheerleaders came for the dedication of George B. Maloof Field.

What They've Said: *"He gave so much of himself to others. I feel he really cared for me and all the other team members. It never seemed to matter whether we won or lost on the scoreboard because when you know the man as a coach and father figure, you know you were a better person for having come under his influence. He was tough, demanding. He asked for 100 percent and he got it. We felt he genuinely loved us and wanted us to become as good as we could be."*

— Chris Eck, member of Maloof's 1984 team

LET'S DON'T FORGET:

Josepy W. Bean. Athletic director and head coach of all sports at Marist from 1904-1932 ... Won football championships in 1922, '25 and '26 ... University of Georgia baseball head coach in 1914-1915 compiling a 33-16-1 record ... Athletic director at the Atlanta Athletic Club from 1910-1949.

H.D. Butler. Head football coach at Decatur High School with a 42-1 mark from 1930-33 ... In 10 seasons (1945-55) at Columbus High School, he recorded 110 victories ... Outstanding athlete at Atlanta's Boys High.

EARL MANN

Long before Ted Turner and the Atlanta Braves, there was "Mr. Atlanta Baseball" and the "Baseball Genius in Dixie."

Mann rose from humble beginnings as a Georgia farm boy to build a baseball dynasty. Born Otis Earl Mann on Oct. 2, 1904, in Riverdale, GA, Mann was selling peanuts, cushions, and soft drinks at Spiller Field (later known as Ponce de Leon Ballpark) by the time he was 12.

After attending Oglethorpe University for a couple of years, Mann sold tickets for the Atlanta Crackers baseball team. He became assistant team secretary in 1924 and eventually was promoted to team secretary, a position he held until 1929. Over the next four years he managed four different minor league teams throughout the South, each of which won a pennant under his leadership. In 1934 he returned to the Atlanta Crackers as vice president. He was named president the following year at age 30, and bought the Crackers outright in 1949.

Mann was among the first minor league operators to send scouts to other ballparks to look for talent. After recruiting a player, Mann paid him between $1,000 and $2,500 up front and wrote into his contract a provision that he would be paid a percentage of what Mann made if his contract was sold to the majors.

Mann's Atlanta Crackers would lead the Southern Association in attendance more times than any other city. His teams also won more league championships than any other Southern Association team. He also was ahead of his time in race relations. In 1949, Mann defied the Ku Klux Klan by hosting Jackie Robinson and the Brooklyn Dodgers to a three-game exhibition series against the Crackers. This was the first time in Atlanta history that blacks and whites competed against each other in a professional sporting contest.

In 1952, Mann also signed the Southern Association's only black ballplayer in history, Atlanta Sports Legend Nat Peeples, to a contract.

Mann was a ballplayer's owner. Universally admired for his generosity, he furnished more players for the majors than any other operator of his era,. But in 1959, after losing money for several consecutive years, Mann turned control of the team's operations over to the Southern Association. He continued to remain active on Atlanta's sports scene, and played an enormous role in Atlanta's development as a world class sports capital.

Mann died on January 6, 1990, and his ashes were spread under the magnolia tree on the site of the former Ponce de Leon Ballpark.

What They've Said: *"I've never met a finer man in all my life."*
— Billie Harden, co-owner of the Atlanta Black Crackers

"I've got no secrets about what success I've had. All I've got to show for it is a lot of long hours and I was putting them in at an age when most kids are only worrying about what they're going to get for Christmas."
— Earl Mann

LET'S DON'T FORGET:

Ralph "Country" Brown. One of the most popular professional baseball players in Atlanta's early sports years, Brown was a member of the minor league Atlanta Crackers from 1947-52. After winning consecutive batting titles and league MVP awards with the Class C Tampa Smokers and AA Augusta Tigers, Brown spent a little time at AAA Newark, only to be demoted to Class A and switched to first base because his arm was too weak. At age 26, he went home to Summerville, in hopes of being traded. Ten days later, Cracker team owner Earl Mann purchased his contract. Brown's salary was $500 a month, and he became one of Atlanta's most popular and beloved players. He led the Southern Association with 33 stolen bases in 1949 and was a member of the 1950 Atlanta Cracker Southern Association championship team. Brown was traded in 1952 to the Chattanooga (Tennessee) Lookouts. He finally retired in 1957, returned to Summerville, and eventually took a job in law enforcement. He died in 1997. Former Georgia governor and U.S. senator Zell Miller has said that Brown was his favorite Atlanta Cracker of all time.

Bob Montag. The Atlanta Crackers own Babe Ruth. "Der Tag" was one of the most popular baseball players in Atlanta history. He never made it to the major leagues, but for countless local baseball fans during the 1950s, he was a bona fide superstar. Montag is the all-time Atlanta Cracker home run leader, hitting 113 round trippers. Thirty nine of those came in 1954, which set the franchise's single season record. One of those home runs landed in a passing train (a set of railroad tracks ran past the Crackers home field, Ponce de Leon Ball Park). A few days later, one of the train's conductors asked Montag to autograph the ball, on which the conductor had written, "Atlanta to Nashville to Atlanta – 518 miles," arguably the longest home run in baseball history.

PETER PRESS MARAVICH

Though his time in Atlanta spanned only four brief years, "Pistol" Pete dazzled the city and the entire NBA with his unparalleled creative offensive talent.

The 1970 College Player of the Year was selected third overall in the NBA draft by the Atlanta Hawks, and wasted little time becoming a prime-time player by averaging 23.2 points per game in his rookie season and making the NBA All-Rookie Team in 1971. Maravich tied an NBA single-game record for most free throws made in one quarter (14) on Nov. 28, 1973, against Buffalo; and most free throws attempted in one quarter (16) on Jan. 2, 1973, against Chicago.

While the Hawks' usually made the playoffs during Maravich's tenure with the team, the squad also was sent home early after the first round was over. In fact, Maravich's first season with the team established the pattern for his years with Atlanta: highly entertaining play and big numbers from "the Pistol," but mediocre seasons and quick playoff exits for the team.

In 1972-73 Maravich led the Hawks to a 46-36 record, the only winning season he would experience in his NBA prime. He earned his first of five All-Star appearances and landed a spot on the All-NBA Second Team by averaging 26.1 points per game. He and fellow Atlanta Sports Legend Lou Hudson comprised a formidable offensive duo, ranking fourth and fifth in the NBA, respectively, but their styles couldn't have been more different. Hudson was an efficient, quiet scoring machine, while Maravich made each basket a spectacle. His passing skills began to pay off and his career-best 6.9 assists per game ranked sixth in the league.

Maravich's final year with Atlanta was his highest-scoring NBA season – and the team's worst during his tenure. He poured in 27.7 points per game in 1973-74, second in the league to Buffalo Braves center Bob McAdoo's 30.6. The Hawks, however, faded to 35-47 and missed the playoffs. Maravich played in his second NBA All-Star Game during the season and scored 15 points in 22 minutes.

After four seasons in Atlanta, Maravich was traded to the New Orleans Jazz where he peaked as an NBA showman and superstar. He made the All-NBA First Team in 1976 and '77 and the All-NBA Second Team again in '78. He led the NBA in scoring in 1977 with a personal high 31.1 points per game.

Maravich finished his career with the Utah Jazz and the Boston Celtics in 1980. In 10 seasons, Maravich scored 15,948 points in 658 games for a 24.2-points-per-game average. His NBA single-game high, a 68-point explosion, came against the New York Knicks on Feb. 25, 1977.

Noted for his mop of brown hair and floppy gray socks, Maravich scored more points in college than any other player in history. In only three years at Louisiana State University, Maravich scored 3,667 points - 1,138 points in 1968, 1,148 in '69 and 1,381 in '70, while averaging 43.8, 44.2 and 44.5 points per game. In the process, "Pistol Pete" set numerous NCAA, SEC and school records and was named a three-time All-America. In his collegiate career, the six-foot-five guard averaged an incredible 44.2 points per game in 83 contests and led the NCAA in scoring three times. He also set an NCAA record by scoring more than 50 points 28 times.

Maravich's retired jersey hangs in the rafters at Philips Arena, home court of the Atlanta Hawks.

BY THE NUMBERS

Collegiate Career
- Louisiana State University (1966-70)
- Three-year letter winner (1967-70)
- The Sporting News College Player of the Year (1970)
- Naismith Award Winner (1970)
- The Sporting News All-America First Team (1968, 1969, 1970)
- Three-time AP and UPI First-Team All-America (1968, 1969, 1970)
- Holds NCAA career record for most points (3,667, 44.2 ppg, three-year career) in 83 games
- Holds NCAA career record for highest points per game average (44.2 ppg)
- Holds NCAA record for most field goals made (1,387) and attempted (3,166)
- Holds NCAA record for most free throws made (893) and attempted (1,152)
- Holds NCAA record for most games scoring at least 50 points (28)
- Holds NCAA single-season record for most points (1,381) and highest per game average (44.5 ppg) in 1970
- Holds NCAA single-season record for most field goals made (522) and attempted (1,668) in 1970
- Holds NCAA single-season record for most games scoring at least 50 points (10) in 1970
- Holds NCAA single-game record for most free throws made (30 of 31) against Oregon State on Dec. 22, 1969
- All-Southeastern Conference (1968, 1969, 1970)

Professional Career
- NBA Atlanta Hawks (1970-74)
- NBA New Orleans Jazz (1974-79)
- NBA Utah Jazz (1979-80)
- NBA Boston Celtics (1979-80)
- All-NBA First Team (1976, 1977)
- All-NBA Second Team (1973, 1978)
- Scored 15,948 points (24.2 points per game) in 658 games
- Led the NBA in scoring (31.1 points per game) in 1977, his career best
- Scored a career-high 68 points (12th best in history) against the New York Knicks on Feb. 25, 1977
- Led the NBA in most field goals attempted in 1974 (1,791) and 1977 (2,047)
- NBA All-Star Team (1973, 1974, 1977, 1978, 1979)
- NBA 50th Anniversary All-Time Team (1996)

LET'S DON'T FORGET:

Dr. Alfred W. Scott. Considered one of the state's best-ever basketball players while at Atlanta Boys High School ... Starred in basketball, football, baseball and track at Boys High from 1912-1915 ... Captained the University of Georgia's 1918 team as a center... Member of the SEC Executive Committee from 1956-1958.

Pat Stephens. Starred at Atlanta Boys High playing four years on the basketball team ... Averaged 20.8 points per game as a senior ... All-State selection in 1923 and led his team to the state title while averaging 20 points per game and scored 284 points during the 14-game season ... Played for the Atlanta Athletic Club (AAC) against college competition ... Helped lead the AAC to a 66-10 record during a six-year span and undefeated marks in 1925-26 and 1929-30 ... Posted a 9-3 record against Georgia and 8-2 against Georgia Tech.

T. MCFERRIN

One of the state's most successful high school football coaches, McFerrin's 34-year career continued when, in March 2009, he became coach of the Jefferson High Dragons, in Jefferson County.

McFerrin's last position before getting back into coaching ended at South Gwinnett where he became only the seventh head coach in Georgia history to win 300 games. To date, his lifetime career record is 301-93-4. He turned South Gwinnett from an 0-10 team in 1997 to 8-5 in 1998 and 9-3 in 1999, building his offense around quarterback David Greene, who became a standout for the University of Georgia.

McFerrin brought South Gwinnett to football prominence in a region dominated by Parkview and Brookwood. He took over South Gwinnett's failing football program in 1998, and turned it into an almost overnight powerhouse. In the first season McFerrin and the Comets went from having a previous 0-10 season to making the Georgia High School AAAA State Playoffs. The team went deep into the playoffs and surprised a lot of the surrounding Gwinnett talent.

With Greene at the helm in 1999, the Comets again made it deep into the Georgia High School AAAAA playoffs, upsetting many state powerhouses along the way. While the 2000 squad finished 3-7, 2001 saw a strong finish, as McFerrin and the Comets went back to the AAAAA state playoffs with a 7-3 record.

In 2002, McFerrin reached the playoffs' second round by upsetting the Cobb County powerhouse, Walton High School, in the first round and losing to Stephenson High School the following week, bringing the Comets overall record to 10-2.

The 2003 season saw yet another successful year, as the Comets captured the Region 8 AAAAA title after going undefeated in the regular season. The 2004 season would prove to be yet another one of McFerrin's fluke seasons, where again the top 10 team from the year before graduated many of its starters. McFerrin and the Comets ended the season 5-5. However during the season the Comets presented McFerrin with his 300th win, a huge honor for the legendary coach. McFerrin retired at the end of a 2004 season, which ended in a 5-5 record, but in which he recorded his 300th win.

In metro Atlanta, McFerrin also held head coaching stints at Lithonia, Forest Park, Peachtree High, and Tucker.

ANTONIO MCKAY

This Atlanta native was a 1984 and 1988 Olympic gold medalist in the men's 4x400 meter relay for the United States, and earned a reputation as one of track's most astute students and outstanding teachers and motivators.

Born in 1964, McKay, while attending Roosevelt High School in Atlanta, was the 400-meter state champion in 1980, '81, and '82. Also in '82, he set the 400-meter state record in 1982 with a time of 46.74, and captured the 1982 state 200-meter title in 21.4 seconds. At Roosevelt High, McKay was a two-time All-State football and 1982 All-State basketball selection.

McKay then enrolled at Georgia Tech, where he was a three-time NCAA All-American and, in 1984, was the NCAA Indoor and Outdoor 400-meter champion.

In 1984, McKay set the indoor 400-meter world record of 45.79 in 1984. During the Olympic trials, he was the 400-meter champion, and during the Games themselves, in Los Angeles, he was a member of the gold-medal winning 1600-meter relay team. McKay also captured the bronze in the 400 meters at the '84 Los Angeles games.

Between the '84 and '88 Olympics, McKay was the 400-meter champion at the 1986 Goodwill Games and, one year later, set the indoor 300-meter world record (32.51) in 1987. After his gold-medal performance as part of the 1600-meter relay team in the 1988 Seoul Olympics, McKay was the 1600-meter relay world indoor champion in 1990.

An eight-time USA Track and Field 400-meter indoor champion, McKay also was the 400-meter World Indoor champion in 1985 and 1987.

LET'S DON'T FORGET:

Ralph Metcalfe. Christened the world's fastest human in 1934 and 1935 ... Atlanta native captured silver in the 100 meters and bronze in the 200 meters at the 1936 Berlin Olympics, and finished just behind the legendary Jesse Owens in the 100 meters ... Held numerous records in the 40- and 200-meter races ... Won the NCAA 100- and 200-meter dashes in 1932 and was the 100- and 220-yard champion in 1933 and '34 ... Won the AAU national 100-yard championship in 1932 and '34, and the 200-meter title from 1932-36 ... Tied the world record of 10.3 in the 100-meter dash eight times ... Tied the 20.6-second world record in the 200-meter ... Retired from competition after the 1936 Olympics ... Served on the Chicago City Council from 1949-71 and was a U.S. Congressman from 1971 until his death in 1978 ... The Ralph H. Metcalfe Federal Building in Chicago is named in his honor.

LARRY MIZE

Despite an outstanding career on the PGA Tour, Mize he is mainly known for just one shot - the chip from off the green at #11, which secured the 1987 Masters.

A Georgia Tech grad, Mize turned professional in 1980. His first PGA Tour win was the 1983 Danny Thomas Memphis Classic.

At the 1987 Masters, Mize was tied with Seve Ballesteros and Greg Norman after four rounds. Ballesteros was eliminated in the first hole of the playoff. On the second playoff hole, which was Augusta's eleventh, a par four, Mize's second shot landed well off the green. Many people assumed that Norman was about to win, but Mize chipped in for a birdie with a sand wedge from around 140 feet. Mize's win was especially appreciated because he is an Augusta native and had even worked on the scoreboard at Augusta's third hole as a teenager. Mize's also came third in the Masters in 1994.

Mize also won four international events and played for the U.S. teams in the Ryder Cup in 1987 and the Dunhill Cup in 2000.

BY THE NUMBERS

PGA NATIONAL WINS
- 1983 Danny Thomas Memphis Classic
- 1987 Masters
- 1993 Northern Telecom Open, Buick Open
- PGA International Wins
- 1988 Casio World Open (Japan Golf Tour)
- 1989 Dunlop Phoenix (Japan Golf Tour)
- 1990 Dunlop Phoenix (Japan Golf Tour)
- 1993 Johnnie Walker World Championship (unofficial PGA event)

JOHNNY MOON

The man whom The Atlanta Constitution in 1970 called "Mr. Sports" coached national amateur men's and women's softball teams that won more than 7,000 games.

An Atlanta native, Moon managed or coached amateur teams over seven decades, including 53 years as a men's softball coach with a record of 2,799-1,051. He coached 19 baseball teams that won 11 city titles and compiled a composite record of 791-231. His girls' basketball Tomboys never had a losing season and won 901 games, and his fast-pitch Tomboys' softball team lasted for 23 seasons and compiled a 612-306 record competing in 17 regional and three nationals.

Moon, a former president of the Southern Major Softball League, was inducted into the Georgia Sports Hall of Fame in 1987, and is a member of the National Softball Hall of Fame.

Moon made softball history in 1990 when – at age 84– he took right field when several of his Charlie's Trading Post players couldn't make it to the Men's Fast Pitch National in Minnesota because of job commitments.

EDWIN MOSES

Winner of two Olympic gold medals in the 400-meter hurdles, Moses was his sport's most dominant figure for more than a decade.

Moses, a native of Ohio, attended Morehouse University in Atlanta on an athletic scholarship. During his famous international 400-meter hurdles career, he won 122 consecutive races over a 10-year span, capturing gold medals at the 1976 Montreal and 1984 Los Angeles Olympics, both in world record time. He won a bronze in 1988, and afterward became a bobsledder for the United States team, which won a bronze at the 1991 World Cup in Germany.

An excellent student, Moses earned a bachelor's degree in physics in 1978 from Morehouse. He later earned his master's degree in business administration from Pepperdine University in Malibu, CA.

Although Moses initially played both basketball and football in high school, he soon turned to and excelled in gymnastics and track. Morehouse had a track team but no track of its own, so Moses used Atlanta public high school facilities to train for the 1976 Olympic trials. He won trials in the 400-meter hurdles, setting a national record of 48.3 seconds, thus making his first Olympic team.

In his first international competition - the 1976 Summer Olympics in Montreal - Moses won gold in the 400-meter hurdles, setting Olympic and world records with a time of 47.63 seconds. But the United States boycotted the 1980 Moscow games, and Moses was forced to wait until the 1984 Los Angeles games to again win gold, becoming only the second man to win two gold medals in the 400-meter hurdles (American Glenn Davis was the first, in 1956 and 1960.)

From August 1977 to May 1987, Moses won 122 consecutive races in his event. In the 1988 Olympics in Seoul, South Korea, Moses ran his fastest Olympic final but finished third to take the bronze medal.

Moses began speaking out against anabolic steroid use in 1983, when he became a member of the Athletics Congress (the former name of USA Track and Field, the country's governing body for the sport), and he eventually led the movement for drug testing to discourage amateur athletes from using the substances.

He is a member of the Atlanta Sports Hall of Fame.

LET'S DON'T FORGET:

Charles Belcher. Born in Decatur, GA ... Set the 600-yard dash world indoor record and also held the southern record in the 440 ... Captured the 440 crown at the Southeastern Conference track championship three years running ... Member of the 1939-40 United States track team ... Set state high school 440-yard dash record at Decatur High School.

DALE MURPHY

One of the best baseball players of the 1980s, Murphy won two Most Valuable Player Awards and clubbed 398 homers while maintaining a hero-like image. An Atlanta Brave from 1976-90, he was one of the most respected and beloved stars of his era. He led the National League in homers, RBIs, and slugging twice each. In his prime he was compared to Joe DiMaggio, Willie Mays, and another Atlanta Sports Legend, Hank Aaron.

Born in Portland, OR, Murphy was the National League MVP and the heart and main cog of the Atlanta Braves' success in the early 1980s. At 6-foot-5 and 215 pounds, Murphy was the Braves catcher for brief periods in 1976 and '77. He became a regular first baseman in '78 and moved to center field because of his speed in 1980.

Known as a great hitter, "Murf" collected four Gold Glove awards for his stellar defensive play. The rangy outfielder led the majors in home runs with 36 in 1984 and 37 in '85. Two years before, he was the majors' RBI leader 109 in 1982 and 121 in '83. He hit .247 or better 11 times with Atlanta and averaged .300 or better in 1977, '83 and '85. Murphy also hit 30 or more home runs six times and blasted 44 in 1987, and led the majors in slugging average in 1983 (.540) and 1984 (.547).

Off the field, Murphy's clean-cut image was an inspiration to many who felt that professional athletes were becoming selfish, spoiled, and self-centered. A devout Mormon and family man, Murphy's nicknames bestowed upon him by teammates reflected that authentic wholesomeness - "Gentle Giant," "John Boy," "Lil' Abner," "All-American Boy," and "Buckethead."

Murphy was drafted by the Braves on June 5, 1974, in the first round of the amateur draft. In 1990, the Braves traded Murphy to the Philadelphia Phillies, where he stayed from 1990-92. His final season came in 1993, with the Colorado Rockies.

In 2007, 'Murph was inducted into the Atlanta Sports Hall of Fame.

What They've Said: *"If you're a coach, you want him as a player. If you're a father, you want him as a son. If you're a woman, you want him as a husband. If you're a kid, you want him as a father. What else can you say about the guy?"*

— Former manager Joe Torre

LARRY NELSON

Born in Fort Payne, AL and growing up in Acworth, GA, Nelson took up golf at the age of 21 after he returned from serving in the infantry in Vietnam. Nelson carefully studied Ben Hogan's book The Five Fundamentals of Golf while learning how to play the game. He soon found that he had a talent for the game, breaking 100 the first time he played and 70 within nine months. He went on to graduate from Kennesaw Junior College in 1970 and turned professional the following year. He qualified for the PGA Tour at 27. His breakthrough year came in 1979 when he won twice and finished second in the money list to Tom Watson.

Nelson won 10 times on the PGA Tour, of which three, a high proportion, were major championships. He earned his first major title at the 1981 PGA Championship which he won by four strokes. In 1983 he was victorious at the U.S. Open at Oakmont, coming from seven behind at the half-way point to defeat Tom Watson by a single shot. Nelson scored a U.S. Open record 65-67 over the last 36 holes at the difficult Oakmont course, which broke a 51 year Open record established by Gene Sarazen. Nelson's 10 under par 132 record score has yet to be equaled. In 1987 he finished tied with Lanny Wadkins after the regulation 72 holes of PGA Championship, and won the title with a par at the first playoff hole.

Nelson played on the U.S. Ryder Cup team in 1979, 1981, and 1987. He also won four tournaments on the Japan Golf Tour.

Nelson was elected to the World Golf Hall of Fame in April 2006, and into the Atlanta Sports Hall of Fame in 2009.

BY THE NUMBERS

- Professional wins: 40
- Number of wins by tour
- PGA Tour: 10
- Japan Golf Tour: 4
- Champions Tour: 19 (tied 10th all time)
- Best results in Major Championships
- The Masters - 5th in 1984
- U.S. Open: Won in 1983
- Open Championship: tied for 12th in 1980
- PGA Championship Won in 1981 and 1987

PHIL NEIKRO

The man known as "Knucksie" was one of the Atlanta Braves' most dominant pitchers and for 21 years, was truly the face of the franchise.

Born in Blaine, Ohio, Niekro fashioned a long, successful sports career by mastering the most confounding pitch in the history of baseball, the knuckleball. His father, a coal miner and pitcher in the Mine Workers League, taught the knuckleball to both of his sons, Phil Jr. and Joe (who also joined the ranks of major league pitchers).

In 1959, after excelling in baseball and basketball in high school, young Phil turned down a college baseball scholarship to sign with the Milwaukee Braves. He slowly advanced through the minor league farm system as a relief pitcher until 1963, when he spent a year in the military.

On April 15, 1964, Niekro made his major league debut as a relief pitcher for the Milwaukee Braves. In 1966 he relocated with the team to Atlanta. The following year, after spending more time in the minor leagues perfecting his knuckleball, the 6-foot-1-inch, 180-pound right-hander became a starting pitcher. At the age of 28, he was a late bloomer on the mound. But he made up for lost time by pitching until he was 48.

The 1997 National Baseball Hall of Famer's all-time career marks include a 318-274 pitching record with a 3.35 lifetime ERA. In his 864 games, he started 716 of them, and pitched 245 complete games. He posted 45 shutouts; 29 saves; and in his 5,404.1 innings he recorded 3,342 strikeouts.

From 1964-83, Niekro's career with the Braves saw him win 268 games with a 3.20 ERA and 2,912 strikeouts. He made five All-Star appearances (four with the Braves), and won five Gold Gloves. His 318 wins ranks him 14th all-time among all major league pitchers.

Niekro also ranks fifth all-time in innings pitched and eighth all-time in strikeouts. He holds or shares 14 Atlanta career pitching records, and won 20 games or more three times and 15 games or more 13 times. His career high in wins came in 1969 with 23. He pitched a no-hitter against San Diego (a 9-0 win) at Atlanta Stadium on Aug. 5, 1973, and later became the oldest pitcher to record a shutout with a four-hit, 8-0 victory in 1985 against Toronto as a New York Yankee.

Niekro was the only pitcher in the major leagues to achieve 300-plus victories by relying almost exclusively on the knuckleball. Unlike other pitches, the knuckleball floats with no spin or rotation, then suddenly dips, dives, or swoops. It's almost impossible not only to hit but also for pitchers to control. Most knuckleball pitchers lose as many games as they win, but Niekro was the exception (along with Hoyt Wilhem, who also pitched into his late 40S). Despite its name, the knuckleball isn't actually thrown with the knuckles. Niekro held the ball so that the first two fingers of his right hand—tips and nails only—touched the top of the ball.

(Continued on next page)

PHIL NEIKRO

Phil and Joe Niekro set a new record for wins (539) by brothers in the major leagues. In addition to pitching, Phil Niekro was also a fine all-around player. Not only was he a five-time Gold Glove winner, but he possessed one of the best right-handed pickoff moves in the game.

Niekro twice he led the National League in wins, and in 1969 he propelled Atlanta to the National League West title with a record of 23-13 (21 complete games, 2.56 ERA). In 1982 Niekro assisted the Braves to another division title during a losing era in which Braves fans rarely found much to cheer about.

After retiring from baseball, Niekro managed Atlanta's AAA farm club at Richmond in 1991. In 1994 he took over the managerial reigns of the Colorado Silver Bullets women's professional baseball team. He is a member of the Atlanta Sports Hall of Fame.

What They've Said:

"Trying to hit him is like trying to eat Jell-O with chopsticks."
— Bobby Murcer

BY THE NUMBERS

CAREER STATISTICS
- Win-Loss record 318-274
- Earned run average 3.35
- Strikeouts 3,342

TEAMS
- Milwaukee / Atlanta Braves (1964-1983, 1987)
- New York Yankees (1984-1985)
- Cleveland Indians (1986-1987)
- Toronto Blue Jays (1987)

CAREER HIGHLIGHTS AND AWARDS
- 5x All-Star selection (1969, 1975, 1978, 1982, 1984)
- 5x Gold Glove Award winner (1978, 1979, 1980, 1982, 1983)
- 1980 Roberto Clemente Award
- 1979 Lou Gehrig Memorial Award
- Atlanta Braves #35 retired

1938 ATLANTA BLACK CRACKERS

Destined to make a run at history, this team was a member of the Negro American League, considered to be the "majors" as far as black baseball was concerned. And if it were not for a most unfortunate series of events, the Black Crackers could have been the city's first major league sporting champion.

Born in the hot, racially charged summer of 1919 as the Atlanta Cubs, the team eventually became known as the Atlanta Black Crackers simply because that's what most people called them because of their familiarity with their white counterparts. They also shared a playing field, and when the white Crackers were playing at Ponce de Leon Ballpark, the Black Crackers were barnstorming all over the South, and often, the nation.

The '38 team included many heralded athletes, including second baseman Gabby Kemp; shortstop Pee Wee Butts; first baseman James "Red" Moore; and sluggers Babe Davis, Don Pelham and Joe "Pig" Greene. Pitchers Bo Mitchell, Eddie "Bullet" Dixon, Felix "Chin" Evens and Twelosh Howard handled most of the mound chores for the club.

But 1938 got off to a rocky start, as the best teams in black baseball (such as the Chicago American Giants, Homestead Grays, Kansas City Monarchs and Indianapolis ABCs) handled the Black Crackers with ease. Halfway during the season, the team was in fourth place, and the ownership took out ads in local newspapers that apologized for the team's poor performance.

As the season's second half got underway, however, the team had turned things around under Kemp, who had been promoted to manager, replacing Vinicus "Nish" Williams. Winning a doubleheader to start the second half, the Black Crackers won 19 consecutive games at one point. Barnstorming throughout the South and Midwest, the team defeated the Memphis Red Sox and Kansas City Monarchs at the end of the year to win the second half of the Negro American League season, thus putting them into the Negro World Series against Memphis.

The team had developed quite a rivalry with Memphis. "The Red Sox had an A-No. 1 ball club, and we had one, and the people came there to see two ballclubs that were rivals tie up as if they were the Yankees and the Dodgers," Kemp said.

But neither team felt they could get a fair shake in each other's ballpark. The Black Crackers had lost eight straight games in Memphis, while the Red Sox had lost five straight in Atlanta. Major R.R. Jackson, president of the Negro American League, ruled that because both teams had failed to show up for scheduled contests because of disagreements and postponements, the playoff series was declared a no-contest.

(Continued on next page)

1938 ATLANTA BLACK CRACKERS

Rumors flew right and left over why the games had been cancelled. Some historians have argued that the teams illegally signed players from each other and other teams as well, while others have said that the umpires assigned to the series were up for sale to the highest bidder. In any event, we'll never know if the Atlanta Black Crackers would have been crowned champions of all of American black baseball during that season. If so, they would have preceded the 1995 Atlanta Braves by more than 50 years.

What They've Said: *"The Black Cracker ballclub was one of the best ballclubs baseball has ever seen in the North or South. That team was well rounded. That was one of the best baseball teams with the best baseball talent, man for man, that I believe has been put together in Atlanta, Georgia, up until the present day."*
— James "Gabby" Kemp

1995 ATLANTA BRAVES

Atlanta's only world championship in any sport came in 1995, when the Braves validated their label as the "Team of the 90's" by winning their first World Series in 38 years.

The Braves also entered the record books as the first franchise to win the World Series in three different cities. Atlanta overcame a 23-20 start (3rd place, 5.0 GB) to post a 67-34 (.663) mark from June 14 through the remainder of the regular season, running away with the National League East title by 21 games. By winning the division with a record of 90-54 (.625), the Braves became the first NL team to finish first in four consecutive completed seasons since the 1921-24 New York Giants.

Atlanta's pitching lived up to expectations, leading the majors with a 3.44 ERA; the Braves' staff became the first to lead the majors in ERA for three straight seasons since the Baltimore Orioles topped the majors from 1969-72.

Greg Maddux claimed his unprecedented fourth straight Cy Young Award, going 19-2 with a 1.63 ERA, becoming the first starting pitcher since Walter Johnson in 1918-19 to record an ERA of less than 1.70 in two consecutive seasons. He ended the season with a major league record 18-game winning streak on the road (including an 0.99 ERA) dating back to July '94.

Mark Wohlers emerged as the dominant closer the Braves had sought throughout the 90's, saving 25 games, including 21 straight chances between May 15 and September 3. Fred McGriff (27), David Justice (24), Ryan Klesko (24) and Rookie of the Year Chipper Jones (23) became the first Braves foursome to hit over 20 homers in a season since 1973, and Javy Lopez matched Joe Torre's 1966 record for the best average by an Atlanta catcher with a .315 mark.

Last at-bat wins were the trademark of the '95 Braves, with Atlanta winning an NL-best 25 games in this fashion, including 18 after July 3. The Braves led the majors with 31 one-run victories, and went on to notch another seven victories in the post-season by one run and/or in their last at bat.

Atlanta beat the Colorado Rockies three games to one in the Division Series, and routed the Reds in the first-ever four-game sweep of an NLCS, before winning the world title with a six-game triumph over the Indians, climaxed by Series MVP Tom Glavine's one-hitter over eight innings and David Justice's decisive sixth-inning homer in the 1-0 finale.

TOMMY NOBIS

ATLANTA FALCONS

Known as "Mr. Falcon" not only for being Atlanta's first-ever draft pick in franchise history but also for his ongoing relationship as an ambassador of goodwill for the team, Nobis was Atlanta's very first professional football hero.

Nobis' collegiate career set a tone for the success he would enjoy as a professional. As a linebacker and offensive guard at the University of Texas, he won both the Outland and Maxwell trophies as best college player, and was twice named an All-American. In 1963, he played on the team that won the 1963 national championship over Navy and its outstanding quarterback, Roger Staubach. In 1964, he was part of a 10-1 squad which beat Alabama and its star quarterback, Joe Namath, in the Orange Bowl.

The San Antonio native was drafted by the expansion Falcons in 1966, and won NFL Rookie of the Year honors. He was also a 1967 and '68 All-NFL pick, and would go on to play in five Pro Bowls.

In nine of his 11 NFL seasons, Nobis led the Falcons in tackles, and his mark of 294 as a rookie is still a club record. He also intercepted 11 passes during his pro career, returning two of them for touchdowns.

After his 46th consecutive NFL game, Nobis underwent knee surgery in 1969 and another one —on the other knee - in 1971. But Nobis came back to earn another Pro Bowl spot in 1972.

In a poll conducted in 1970 by ABC to pick the best athlete of the decade of the 1960s, Nobis came in second behind running back O.J. Simpson.

The list of honors accorded Nobis is lengthy indeed. Besides being a member of the Atlanta Sports Hall of Fame inaugural class, he is enshrined in the National Football Foundation Hall of Fame; the Texas Hall of Fame; the Georgia Hall of Fame; and the College Football Hall of Fame. He was also named to *Sports Illustrated's* All-Century Team (1869-1969).

Nobis' off-the-field activities have garnered him as much attention as he gained during his playing career. Nobis is founder and board member of the Tommy Nobis Center, which provides job training and employment services for both youth and adults with disabilities. The center has been in place for more than 27 years and its staff has placed more than 12,000 young people and adults into jobs throughout metro Atlanta.

Nobis also has been named NFL Man of the Year, in addition to receiving the Joseph P. Kennedy award for Special Olympics. His No. 60 jersey was one of those the Falcons' honored in its inaugural Ring of Honor ceremony in 2004.

What They've Said: *"When you attended a Falcons game in the '60s, you could be certain that the team would be outclassed at every position but linebacker, where Nobis was in a class by himself. When his team was trailing by 40 or more points, Nobis hit with as much devastation as if the game depended on it."*
— Gene Asher, writer

LET'S DON'T FORGET:

Walker G. "Bix Six" Carpenter. 1917 Georgia Tech All-American who helped lead the Yellow Jackets to the 1917 National Championship ... Tech went 9-0 that season and outscored opponents 491-17 ... Member of the Helms Football Hall of fame and Georgia Tech Hall of Fame.

JESSE LAMAR OUTLAR

For 28 years Outlar was sports editor and columnist for *The Atlanta Constitution*, part of a career that spanned 41 years with the newspaper. The National Sportswriters and Sportscasters Association named Outlar as Georgia Sportswriter of the Year three times, and the Associated Press voted him Georgia's Sports Columnist of the Year four times.

Outlar, a native Georgian and University of Georgia graduate, wrote two books - "Between the Hedges" and "Caught Short." He twice served as president of the Atlanta chapter of the Baseball Writers Association of America, and also played a crucial role in Atlanta's development as a major league sports city when he served on the Stadium Authority when the brand new Atlanta Stadium was built in the mid-1960s.

Outlar covered virtually every major event in the world of sports – high school, college and professional football and baseball; the Kentucky Derby; the Super Bowl; the World Series; the Masters; fellow Atlanta Sports Legend Henry Aaron's home-run chase of the Babe; Georgia winning the college football championship; and his favorite, Georgia's breaking of its eight-year drought against Georgia Tech.

On Oct. 7, 1983, after covering a Falcons' afternoon home game, Outlar was approaching his car when he was shot at almost point-blank range by a robber. He recovered from the close call, and no one was ever charged with the crime.

Arguably Outlar's biggest scoop came when he predicted the NFL would award Atlanta a franchise, when only the day before, *The Atlanta Journal* said the American Football League would award the city a team.

"Nobody understood the nuts and bolts better than Jesse and nobody made sportswriting more fun."
— Edwin Pope, "The Miami Herald"

WILLIAM PORTER PAYNE

On Feb. 9, 1987, Billy Payne came home from church and told his wife he'd decided to bring the Olympics to Atlanta.

Just like that.

Rarely has anyone come up with an idea so universally considered as far-fetched (and that's putting it mildly) by so many. But rarely has anyone demonstrated the tenacity, determination and dedication to make so many people believe that anything, indeed, is possible, if you're willing to pay the price, than Payne.

A decade of Payne's life went into the 1996 Atlanta Games. From conception and fundraising to actually putting on the Olympics, Payne was front and center. And there was a price to be paid. Payne battled local officials who had their own pork barrel agendas. As the date of the actual Games was approaching, Payne was forced to undergo major heart surgery. And in the middle of the Games themselves, a bomb went off in Centennial Park, killing two and injuring dozens.

Through it all, Payne maintained a positive, public image of composure and dignity, and now will always be able to say that his city hosted history's largest peacetime gathering of Olympic athletes and spectators.

Payne was born in Athens, GA, and was an outstanding college football player at the University of Georgia. In 1968 he was an All-SEC selection at defensive end, and was a three-year football letterman from 1966-68.

Payne's campus honors foretold his later achievements. He served as vice president of the student government as a sophomore, and was named an academic all-American. He received an NCAA postgraduate scholarship and a National Football Hall of Fame postgraduate fellowship.

After graduating from Georgia in 1969 with honors and a degree in political science, Payne continued his studies at Georgia's Joseph Henry Lumpkin School of Law, where he earned his law degree in 1973. Later, Payne was involved in all phases of a successful private law practice, specializing in real estate law in Atlanta until 1988.

From the very beginning, Payne enlisted the support of Atlanta's foremost business, civic and political leaders to become the 1996 Olympic host city. Payne headed the Atlanta Organizing Committee and directed the activities of that committee in preparing Atlanta's bid. In 1991, he became co-chairman of the Atlanta Centennial Olympic Properties. When the International Olympic Committee (IOC) named Atlanta as 1996 host city, he became president of the Atlanta Committee for the Olympic Games. Payne thus became the first person in modern Olympic history to lead a bid effort and continue uninterrupted as president of an Olympic organizing committee.

(Continued on next page)

WILLIAM PORTER PAYNE

Through it all, Payne and his team picked up things as they went along. After the city had been chosen as the elected U.S. representative, Payne came back to Atlanta with little or no knowledge of how to bid for the Olympics on an international basis. He had to learn about Olympic protocol when it came to dealing with members of the IOC.

Payne faced challenges at home as well. Once Atlanta was chosen as the official site, everyone wanted a piece of the Olympic action, and the city's image was tarnished by political corruption and unbridled, shameless economic exploitation.

But through Payne's effort and sacrifice, Atlanta's infrastructure was transformed, and the city continues enjoying major new sporting venues, expanded housing options, better highways and modern transportation technology.

Just like that.

On May 5, 2006, Payne replaced Hootie Johnson as chairman of Augusta National Golf Club, home of the Masters Tournament. As chairman, Payne has already made some adjustments at the Masters, including a new television contract with *ESPN* that allowed for coverage of the par-3 tournament in 2008.

BY THE NUMBERS

The 1996 Centennial Olympic Games

- 197 nations
- 10,318 athletes (3,512 women, 6,806 men)
- 271 events
- 47,466 volunteers
- 15,108 media (5,695 written press, 9,413 broadcasters)
- Opening date: July 19, 1996
- Closing date: August 4, 1996

NAT PEEPLES

Peeples may have walked a harder road than Jackie Robinson's, because he would be destined to break the athletics color barrier in the deep South, all the while turning the other cheek in Robinson-esque fashion.

Peeples was the first black player signed by the Atlanta Crackers, and the only one during the Southern Association's 61-year existence. Atlanta Sports Legend Earl Mann signed Peeples for the 1954 team, arguably one of the greatest to ever wear the Cracker uniform. Peeples set the '54 preseason on fire, batting over .400. But he only played in one regular season game, and was optioned to a Class-A franchise only two weeks into the regular season.

Born June 26, 1926, Peeples' career began in 1948, when he dropped out of LeMoyne College to play for his hometown Memphis Red Sox. One year later, he signed with the Kansas City Monarchs and caught for the legendary Satchel Paige himself. He also met and played with James Thomas "Cool Papa" Bell. Peeples and the Monarchs competed against the greatest Negro American League teams of the era, including the Chicago-American Giants, Homestead Grays and Cleveland Buckeyes. A right-handed catcher and outfielder, he hit .302 in 1950 during a split season playing for both the Monarchs and the Indianapolis Clowns.

By the early 1950s, and encouraged by the minor league success of such future stars as Henry Aaron, Felix Mantilla and Horace Garner, Mann believed the time was ripe for a black ballplayer in the South. Peeples' spring training camp and preseason were outstanding. In his first game, he hit a pinch-hit double, and a single and a double the next. Three games later, he blasted a 400-foot home run. He arrived in Atlanta – for two weeks of exhibitions before the '54 regular season began – hitting .416.

Almost 7,000 people gave Peeples a courteous welcome for his first exhibition game at Ponce de Leon Ballpark, when the Crackers hosted the major league Milwaukee Braves. The Braves would have posted a no-hitter had it not been for Peeples, who got the Crackers' only hit of the game. Peeples finished the preseason hitting .333, with six homers in 48 at-bats.

Peeples made only one regular season appearance for the Crackers, in the second game of the year, against the Bears in Mobile. Two weeks later, Mann sent him down to Class A Jacksonville (the Crackers were a Double-A team at the time), with the explanation that Peeples needed to be on a team in which he could play on a daily basis.

(Continued on next page)

NAT PEEPLES

It's true that the '54 Cracker team was loaded with talent, and would set numerous all-time league records that year. However, laws in Alabama and Louisiana prohibited blacks and whites from competing against each other, and speculation continues that had club owners in those states allowed Peeples and the Crackers to compete in their ballparks, the owners and general managers of those clubs may have subjected themselves to jail time.

Life went on for Peeples, who played 94 games in Jacksonville to finish out the year at .288. He bounced around the Braves' farm system over the next five years, rising as high as Triple A. He also played winter ball in Colombia, Venezuela, Cuba and Panama. In 1960 the Braves sold his contract to the Mexico City Reds of the Mexican League, where his career ended in the middle of a .429 hitting streak. Chasing down a fly ball in a baseball park that had been converted from a football stadium, Peeples stepped into a hole and tore numerous ligaments in his knee. Carried off the field on a stretcher, Peeples was never able to run again.

What They've Said: *"I never understood why Atlanta wanted me. We had other black players in the farm system who were better than me. But when I signed, Earl Mann said my job would be harder than Jackie Robinson's because I'd have to play in the South."*
— Nat Peeples

LET'S DON'T FORGET:

David Justice. As a Brave, he hit the only home run in game six of the 1995 World Series and give the franchise its first world championship in Atlanta ... An outspoken lefthanded outfielder who could hit both for average and power ... Rarely reached 500 at-bats in a season, and was subject to rumors that he was injury-prone ... His teams went to the playoffs every year between 1991 and 2000, except 1996 ... His other world championship came in 2000 with the New York Yankees ... Inducted into the Atlanta Braves Hall of Fame.

GARLAND PINHOLSTER

The man who molded Oglethorpe University into one of the most successful basketball programs in the country compiled a 181-67 record at Oglethorpe from 1956-66 and was 276-89 throughout his entire college coaching career.

Pinholster coached the 1963 United States Pan American team to the gold medal with NBA great Willis Reed playing for him. The innovator of the "wheel offense" at Oglethorpe, his teams led the nation in defense four years, and they were the first to use the huddle on the floor prior to foul shots.

Ever the originator of new ideas and techniques, Pinholster popularized the use of hand signals to conserve time outs. He advocated summer basketball camps in Georgia, and perhaps his most famous victory was when he led Oglethorpe to a victory over Southern Illinois (student body 23,000) while Oglethorpe had a student body of only 425.

Pinholster revived the Oglethorpe basketball program with no budget in 1956, scraping up money from boosters and picking out players at random in the dorm. He had a winning record by his second year. In 1963, he took the Stormy Petrels to the semifinals of the NCAA Division II tournament and coached the U.S. team to the gold medal in the Pan American Games. His personal fame grew as he wrote five books on coaching for a major publisher.

"Garland Pinholster, for a period of time, was the best coach in the United States."

— Gary Colson, former head coach at Valdosta State, Pepperdine, New Mexico and Fresno State

LET'S DON'T FORGET:

Stephen J. Schmidt, Sr. First chairman of his alma mater, Oglethorpe University Athletic Committee ... Stock holder of Atlanta Crackers ... Member of the Oglethorpe University Hall of Fame ... Founding father and early president of Braves 400 Club and Atlanta Tipoff Club ... Organized a memorial for the late Atlanta Sports Legend Earl Mann after Mann's death. The service was held beneath the magnolia tree in the former Ponce de Leon Ball Park. Schmidt's company, Dixie Stamp & Seal, handed out hundreds of red, white and blue Cracker license plates.

CHARLES ABNER POWELL

One of the most colorful and charismatic figures in baseball history, Powell is the man responsible for the birth of Atlanta's very first sports dynasty.

"Ab" Powell – a pitcher, catcher, infielder and outfielder, all in one package – played two years in the majors, with Washington in the Union Association (1884) and the American Association's Baltimore and Cincinnati teams in 1886. He went to New Orleans in 1887, as owner/manager of the Southern League's Pelicans. Because of the Crescent City's frequent rains, he devised the idea both of covering the infield with a tarpaulin during downpours and a system whereby fans with tickets to rained-out games kept their stub for re-admittance to a later contest – the rain check.

He also convinced other club owners that, on a certain day of the week, women should be admitted into the ballpark at half price or free. Thus, Ladies' Day.

In 1900, as one of the organizers of the new Southern Association, Powell was co-owner of a team in Selma, Ala., the Christians, along with his New Orleans Pelicans. Both teams finished dismally, and in 1901, Powell moved his Selma team (which had finished dead last at 37-78) to Atlanta, christening them the Crackers.

Powell sold the Crackers in 1905 for $20,000. Powell would become the Southern Association's "grand old man" as he kept a keen interest in the circuit up to the time of his death in 1953 at the age of 92.

And the team he brought to Atlanta would set the stage for the city's championship baseball tradition. From 1901-65, the Crackers would become the most successful minor league team in baseball history, winning 17 league championships over that period. Only the New York Yankees posted a better pennant-winning record during that time.

LET'S DON'T FORGET:

The 1885 Atlanta Baseball Team. Atlanta's first official minor league professional baseball team ... Part of the original Southern League circuit ... Won the first Southern League pennant in 1885 with a record of 60-31, becoming Atlanta's and the South's first professional sports championship team.

MARK PRICE

One of the best free-throw shooters in NBA history, Price excelled in the pros for 12 years. One of only six players in Yellow Jacket basketball history to have his jersey retired, Price made 90.4 percent of his free-throws in his NBA career.

Price's father was an Oklahoma basketball hero who starred on the Norman High School basketball team and for the University of Oklahoma. In 1982 Price, a graduate of Enid High School, was named the Oklahoman high school player of the year. He tied his father's state tournament scoring record with 42 points in the first round of the 1982 tournament. Price led his state class in scoring his junior and senior seasons.

Price left Oklahoma after high school to play college basketball at Georgia Tech. While there, he led the Atlantic Coast Conference in scoring as a freshman over Michael Jordan. He made the All-Conference team three times and ended his Georgia Tech stint as their second all-time scorer.

The Dallas Mavericks selected Price in the second round of the 1986 NBA draft and traded him to the Cleveland Cavaliers. Price holds many Cleveland franchise career records (assists, steals, free throw percentage, and three-point field goals made and attempted). In 1995 Cleveland traded him to the Washington Bullets, now the Wizards. In 1996 the Golden State Warriors signed Price and then traded him to the Orlando Magic in 1997, where he played his final season.

Price was known as one of the league's most consistent shooters. He finished his career with a 90.4 percent free throw shooting percentage, placing him as the league's all-time leader in this statistical area, and a 40 percent three-point field goal shooting percentage During the 1988-89 season, Price became the third player, along with Larry Bird and Reggie Miller, to shoot at least 40 percent from three-point range, at least 50 percent from the field and at least 90 percent from the free throw line.

Price played for the US national team in the 1994 FIBA World Championship, winning the gold medal.

Price averaged 15.2 points and 6.7 assists for his entire career and achieved All-Star status four of his 12 professional years. Besides his prowess at the free-throw line, Price made over 40 percent of his three-point shots. He scored more than 10,000 points and won the NBA long distance shootout twice on All-Star weekend.

After retiring from the NBA in 1998, Price and his family settled in Georgia where he coached basketball. Not long after his retirement, Cleveland retired his number 25.

BY THE NUMBERS

College Georgia Tech

Draft 2nd round, 25th overall, 1986 Dallas Mavericks

Pro career 1986–1998, 4-Time NBA All-Star

Former teams Cleveland Cavaliers (1986-1995), Washington Bullets (1995-1996), Golden State Warriors (1996-1997), Orlando Magic (1997-1998)

DAN REEVES

He did what few people, in their wildest dreams, thought possible – take the Atlanta Falcons to the Super Bowl.

In 1997, Reeves took over a professional football franchise more often associated with hapless futility than success and, one year later, not only led it to its best regular season record (14-2), but also the NFL's title game. Mentored in the ways of legendary Dallas Cowboys head coach Tom Landry, Reeves brought a sense of professionalism, organization and class to the team, and played central roles in drafting players.

Born in Rome, GA, Reeves' collegiate career at the University of South Carolina was highlighted by two All-ACC quarterback appearances, in 1962 and 1964. As an 18-year-old sophomore in 1962, Reeves was the youngest starting QB in major college football at the time.

In the pros, Reeves enjoyed an incredible career - both on the field and on the sidelines. From 1965-72, Reeves played with the Cowboys as an all-purpose back, and was a member of the Super Bowl VI championship team. He rushed for 1,990 yards and 25 touchdowns and also caught 129 passes for 1,693 yards and 17 TDs during his playing career.

Reeves became a head coach for the first time in 1981, with the Denver Broncos, and led the Rocky Mountain franchise to Super Bowls XXI, XXII and XXIV, with Hall of Fame quarterback John Elway under center. He then moved to the Big Apple, coaching the New York Giants for four years before returning home to his native Georgia as head coach of the Falcons.

Reeves first year at the Falcon helm resulted in a 7-9 record, a marked improvement over the previous year's 3-13 mark. In 1998, Reeves charted the Falcons to the NFC championship, when the Falcons defeated the heavily favored Minnesota Vikings – in Minnesota – by a score of 30-27. The Falcons faced Reeves' old team – the Broncos – and quarterback – Elway – losing by a score of 34-19.

High hopes abounded for the Falcons in 1999, hopes that were dashed by a rash of injuries. In 2001, however, Reeves and the Falcons made a blockbuster draft day move, sending three future draft picks and a player to the San Diego Chargers in exchange for the Chargers' No. 1 draft spot, which they then used to select quarterback Michael Vick. The Virginia Tech star quickly earned a reputation as the league's most exciting and electrifying player, and in 2002, Reeves, Vick and the Falcons not only came within one game of the NFC championship game, they also handed the Green Bay Packers their first home playoff loss in history.

During his final years with the Falcons, Reeves was the NFL's winningest active coach. He was Coach of the Year five times (1984, '89, '91, '93, and '98), participating in 48 playoff games and nine Super Bowls as an NFL player and coach.

After his career with the Falcons, Reeves played a major role in generating support for Georgia State University's new collegiate football program.

BY THE NUMBERS
DAN REEVES PROFESSIONAL COACHING RECORD

Year	TM	Reg. Season W	L	T	Playoffs W	L
1981	DEN	10	6	0	0	0
1982	DEN	2	7	0	0	0
1983	DEN	9	7	0	0	1
1984	DEN	13	3	0	0	1
1985	DEN	11	5	0	0	0
1986	DEN	11	5	0	2	1
1987	DEN	10	4	1	2	1
1988	DEN	8	8	0	0	0
1989	DEN	11	5	0	2	1
1990	DEN	5	11	0	0	0
1991	DEN	12	4	0	1	1
1992	DEN	8	8	0	0	0
1993	NYG	11	5	0	1	1
1994	NYG	9	7	0	0	0
1995	NYG	5	11	0	0	0
1996	NYG	6	10	0	0	0
1997	ATL	7	9	0	0	0
1998	ATL	14	2	0	2	1
1999	ATL	5	11	0	0	0
2000	ATL	4	12	0	0	0
2001	ATL	7	9	0	0	0
2002	ATL	9	6	1	1	1
2003	ATL	3	10	0	0	0
TOTALS		**190**	**165**	**2**	**11**	**9**

LET'S DON'T FORGET:

Paul A. Duke. Atlanta native who came out of nowhere as a walk-on freshman at Georgia Tech and finished his career as an All-American ... Chosen All-American in 1946 as a center by six different services (AP, UPI, NEA, Colliers, All-American Board & American Football Coaches Association) ... First-team All-SEC (AP) ... Atlanta Touchdown Club's SEC Lineman of the Year ... Captained Bobby Dodd's first Tech team ... Played one season with the N.Y. Yankees of the American Football Conference ... Played only one year of high school football at Atlanta Boys High after attending Druid Hills, which did not field a team.

Pete Brown. Struggled for two football seasons as fullback and linebacker at Georgia Tech before emerging as 1952 AP All-American offensive center ... Played at center over two-year period (1951-52) as Bobby Dodd's Yellow Jackets completed their finest two-season span ever with a 33-0-1 record which included a 17-14 Orange Bowl victory over Baylor and 24-7 Sugar Bowl win against Ole Miss ... Considered one of Tech's best-ever blocking centers ... Three-year letterman from 1950-52 ... One of six Yellow Jackets to be named to All-American teams and one of four to be chosen to play in the 1953 College All-Star game in Chicago ...1st team All-SEC (AP) and 2nd team All-SEC (UPI) ... Lettered three times in baseball as outfielder and track as a high jumper ... Also a strong competitor in all the dash events ... Played pro football as center, linebacker and punter for the San Francisco 49ers (1953-54) and the Canadian Football League's Vancouver British Columbia Lions (1958).

RANDY RHINO

Georgia Tech's first three-time first-team All-American, Rhino gained a lot of national attention when he appeared in a photo shoot with, yes, a rhino.

But Rhino's Tech career was filled with far more impact than a simple magazine shot. A defensive back and return specialist, Rhino earned first-team all-America honors three straight years from 1972-74, including consensus first-team accolades in '73. He also was named all-Southeast Independent all three years and participated in the Blue-Gray Game and Hula Bowl following his senior season.

Rhino made 14 career interceptions, which still ranks second in Georgia Tech history. He averaged 13.1 yards per punt return in his career for a total of 749 yards, which remains a Rambling Wreck record. He also holds the school record for longest punt return with a 96-yarder against South Carolina in 1972, while his Tech season record of 441 punt return yards in 1972 was eventually broken by his son, Kelley.

Rhino set numerous other records with the Ramblin' Wreck: most TD-saving tackles in a season (11); most interceptions in a game (3) and career (14); most net yards in punt returns season (441) and career (749); career punt return average (13.1); career kickoff returns (37); most yards kickoff returns season (425) and career (870).

Rhino was honored as Georgia Amateur Athlete of the Year in 1972 by the Georgia Sports Hall of Fame. He was drafted by the NFL's New Orleans Saints and played a four-game stint with the Charlotte Hornets of the World Football League. Rhino also played in the Canadian Football League with the Montreal Alouettes (1974-80) and Ottawa Roughriders (1981).

Rhino became the CFL's all-time career punt-return and total yards leader, and helped lead the Alouettes to the CFL championship in 1977. He was selected All-Pro at Montreal in 1977, '78 and '81, and he earned the 1978 Schenley Award as the Eastern Conference's Outstanding Defensive Player. As a pro, he also led the CFL in punt returns three years.

LET'S DON'T FORGET:

The Rhino Family. A name synonymous with Georgia Tech football ... Father Chappell Rhino played for the Yellow Jackets in the '50s under Atlanta Sports Legend Bobby Dodd ... Son Kelley was an all-Atlantic Coast Conference punt return specialist for the Jackets ... Brother Danny also lettered for Tech from 1974-76.

Robert T. Davis, Jr. An All-American and All-SEC lineman for Georgia Tech in 1947 ... Selected All-SEC in 1945 and '46 ... Captained the '46 football team ... Chosen 1947 SEC Lineman of the Year by the Atlanta Touchdown Club ... Drafted in '47 by Buffalo of the All American Football Conference in the second round and the NFL New York Giants in the fourth round ... Played the '48 NFL season for the Boston Yanks ... Four-year letterman in football and three-year basketball letterman ... Started on the 1945 and '46 basketball teams averaging 6.4 points per game at the pivot position in '45.

George Matthews. Four-year Georgia Tech football and one-year basketball letterman ... Member of the Georgia Tech Hall of Fame ... Drafted by the NFL's New York Giants.

DR. HOMER RICE

One of the nation's most respected collegiate administrators, Rice saw Georgia Tech sports reach a new level of success on and off the playing field.

After inheriting an athletics infrastructure that was considered among the ACC's worst in 1981, Rice left a legacy of impressive athletics facilities, successful sports, big-name coaches and successful student-athletes.

Under Rice's leadership, Georgia Tech became one of the few technically oriented universities in the nation to successfully compete at the Division I level in sports. Under Rice, Tech sports programs achieved No. 1 rankings in football, basketball, baseball and golf; a Final Four appearance in 1990 and five Sweet 16 appearances in men's basketball; an N.W.I.T. championship for the Lady Jackets in basketball in 1992; 17 ACC Coach of the Year and 17 ACC Player of the Year winners; and three Olympic medalists in track, including four gold medals.

Rice enjoyed a distinguished career in coaching and athletics management since his beginning as a high school football coach in 1951. His collegiate coaching career covered Kentucky, Oklahoma, Cincinnati and Rice University. He later became head coach of the Cincinnati Bengals, and served as athletics director at three major universities - North Carolina (1969-75); Rice (1976-77); and Georgia Tech (1980-97).

Rice developed the acclaimed Total Person Concept in the 1980s and used it to mold a generation of athletes who excelled in the classroom, on the field and in life. It has served as the model for more than 170 schools around the country and is the basis of the NCAA "CHAMPS" program.

Rice's colleagues in the National Association of Collegiate Directors of Athletics established the Homer Rice Award to honor the athletics director or conference commissioner who most contributes to exemplary service to college athletic. Rice served as president of the NACD; chairman of the NCAA Football Rules Committee; chairman of the NCAA Television Committee; and chairman of the ACC Rules Committee.

Rice at first was reluctant to come to Tech. In fact, before his arrival, there had been meetings to discuss whether Tech should disband football, or perhaps move to a Division III program with no scholarships. Administrators also were considering whether the school's entire sports program should be dismantled.

Tech President Joseph M. Pettit had tried to lure the 53-year-old Rice to Atlanta on three previous occasions. On the fourth attempt, Pettit enlisted the support of legendary Tech coach Bobby Dodd.

Once on the Tech campus, Rice's first hire was an unknown basketball coach from Appalachian State – Bobby Cremins – who would lead Tech's men's basketball into national prominence. Football coach Bill Curry posted a winning record in 1982, and Rice brought in Jim Morris to take over a fairly well-established baseball program with orders to take it to the next level.

(Continued on next page)

DR. HOMER RICE

Georgia Tech began a climb that would eventually bring it a national championship in football and 15 ACC team championships - one in football, three in basketball, five in baseball, five in golf and one in volleyball. Tech's athletics budget jumped from $2.5 million to $19 million, and its self-esteem on the athletic field jumped even higher.

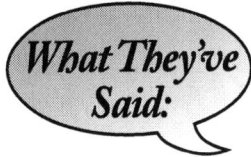

"Heisman, Alexander, Dodd, Ross, and now Rice. Those are some of the outstanding names associated with Georgia Tech athletics. And it is indeed select company Homer Rice joins in the annals of Georgia Tech athletics. Like those other greats before him, this man has left an indelible mark on Georgia Tech."

— Former Georgia Tech President Wayne Clough

LET'S DON'T FORGET:

Leonidas S. Epps. Tallied a 424-264 record as head basketball coach at Clark College in Atlanta ... Clark's head football coach from 1951-70 ... Also coached golf, tennis and track ... Served as athletic director at Clark for 30 years ... Member of the Atlanta University Hall of Fame

PAUL RAPIER RICHARDS

Richards' impact on Atlanta baseball was felt at both the major and minor league levels.

As manager of the Southern Association's Atlanta Crackers in the late 1930s and early '40s, Richards posted a 190-117 record. His 1938 and '41 clubs won the Southern Association championships, and the '41 club was once referred to by Atlanta Sports Legend Earl Mann, the team's owner and general manager, as his all-time favorite. Richards was also vice president of the major league Braves from 1966, when the team moved to Atlanta from Milwaukee, until 1972.

Richards' managerial career began while he was playing on the field. He was a catcher and right-handed batter with the Brooklyn Dodgers (1932); New York Giants (1933-35); and Philadelphia Athletics (1935). Then he landed the Atlanta job; and from 1943-46, the Detroit Tigers, where, in '45, he was a member of its world championship team. After retiring from the field of play, Richards became the manager of the Chicago White Sox (1951-54, 1976) and Baltimore Orioles (1955-61).

Richards became a successful big-league manager with the White Sox in 1951, with four winning seasons, but his club always finished behind the Yankees ('51, '52, '53) and Indians ('54). With the Orioles, he served as both field manager and GM through 1958. After 1959, Richards served strictly as the O's field manager through mid-September 1961.

As a GM, Richards concentrated on signing good defensive players (such as Brooks Robinson) and hard-throwing young pitchers (such as Steve Barber, Milt Pappas and Chuck Estrada). The O's finally blossomed in 1960 with a second place finish after five disappointing seasons.

A year later, Richards resigned as Orioles manager to become GM of the new Houston Colt .45s National League club. Richards stocked the Houston club (soon renamed the Astros) with young players - including Joe Morgan, Jimmy Wynn, Don Wilson and Rusty Staub - but he was fired after the '65 season when the on-field results did not match ownership's expectations.

The following year, Richards was hired as director of player personnel by the Atlanta Braves. By the end of the '66 season, Richards was given the title of GM.

Richards' six years at Atlanta's helm were in some ways his most successful in baseball: his 1969 Braves, skippered by his longtime protégé Luman Harris, won the National League West title. But that team was swept by the eventual world champion "Miracle Mets" in the first National League Championship Series ever played.

The Braves failed to contend in 1970 and '71. Unable to reinvigorate the system with young players, as he had done in Baltimore and Houston, Richards was fired in '72. He made a brief comeback as manager of the White Sox in 1976. He died in 1986 at the age of 77.

(Continued on next page)

PAUL RAPIER RICHARDS

BY THE NUMBERS

TEAMS

Player
- Brooklyn Dodgers (1932)
- New York Giants (1933-1935)
- Philadelphia Athletics (1935)
- Detroit Tigers (1943-1946)

Manager
- Chicago White Sox (1951-1954)
- Baltimore Orioles (1955-1961)
- Chicago White Sox (1976)
- Career highlights and awards
- 1945 World Series Championship

LET'S DON'T FORGET:

Hugh Casey. Atlanta native who played for the Chicago Cubs (1935), Brooklyn Dodgers (1939-48), Pittsburgh Pirates (1949) and New York Yankees (1949) posting a career mark of 75-42 (.641 winning percentage) with a 3.45 ERA and 55 saves ... 51 of his career wins came in relief ... Pitched in four World Series games with a 2-2 record and 1.72 ERA in 15.2 innings for the Dodgers ... Posted back-to-back victories in the 1947 World Series against the New York Yankees (0.87 ERA) ... Led the league in saves in 1941 (13), and 1947 (18) ... Won 10 or more games in five seasons ... "He was a real good friend, the nicest guy you would ever want to meet. But on that mound, [he] had a mean streak. He just as soon knock down a hitter as look at him." *Whitlow Wyatt*

PEPPER RODGERS

One of the most colorful and quotable college football coaches of his era, Rodgers also was one of the most successful, guiding Georgia Tech to four winning seasons during his six years on The Flats.

An Atlanta native, Rodger's overall collegiate coaching record is 73-65-2, from 1967-79. His first stint as a head football came at Kansas from 1967-'70, where he revived a dying Jayhawk program. He led the school to the Big Eight Conference championship (9-2) and a berth in the Orange Bowl where it lost a one-point heartbreaker to Penn State, 15-14.

Rodgers' first team in 1967 placed second in the Big Eight with a 5-2 conference record. He was Big Eight Coach of the Year in 1967, and produced a 20-22 record in his four seasons at Kansas, where he coached future NFL stars Bobby Douglas (quarterback), John Zook (defensive end) and John Riggins (NFL Hall of Fame running back).

From there, Rodgers went to UCLA from 1971-73, fashioning a 19-12-1 record. He guided the Bruins to an 8-3 mark in '72 and 9-2 in '73, and his teams led the Pac-Eight in rushing and ranked second nationally in '72. UCLA's high-powered '73 offense led the nation in rushing, ranking second in scoring and third in total offense.

In 1974, Rodgers came home to Georgia Tech. He earned Southern Independent Coach of the Year honors in 1974, and coached five All-Americans including first-team picks (and Atlanta Sports Legend) Randy Rhino, Lucius Sanford, and Don Bessillieu. Two dozen of his players were NFL draft picks, with Eddie Lee Ivery and Kent Hill taken in the first-round (1978).

Rodgers' best season came in '78 as the Yellow Jackets went 7-5 and earned a berth in the Peach Bowl. Ivery broke the NCAA single game rushing record with 356 yards against Air Force in 1978, and one of Rodgers biggest victories as a college coach came in '76 when Tech upset 11th-ranked Notre Dame, 23-14, without throwing a pass.

In the pros, Rodgers later coached the USFL Memphis Showboats (1978) and the Memphis Mad Dogs of the CFL (1995).

LET'S DON'T FORGET:

Allen Ralph "Buck" Flowers. Georgia Tech football All-American in 1918 and '20 ... All-Southern Conference pick in 1919 and '20 ... Member of the Atlanta Touchdown Club's Southeastern Area All-Time Team (1869-1919) ... Captain and four-year Tech football letterman ... Member of the Georgia Tech and College Football Halls of Fame.

George A. Morris, Jr. Co-Captain of Georgia Tech's 1952 national championship team ... 1952 first-team All-American and All-SEC ... Second-team All-SEC in '51 ... GTE Academic All-American in '52 ... Inducted into the College Football Hall of Fame and Georgia Tech Hall of Fame ... Played one season in the NFL with the San Francisco 49ers in 1956 ... Head SEC linesman (official) for 20 years.

Henry R. "Peter" Pund. 1928 All-American at Georgia Tech ... 1927 and '28 All-Southern Conference selection ... Led Tech to a 10-0 record and an 8-7 Rose Bowl victory ... Captain and three-year letterman for the Yellow Jackets ... Member of the Georgia Tech and College Football Halls of Fame.

BOBBY ROSS

In his five years as Georgia Tech's head football coach, Ross restored the Tech program to national prominence, highlighted by its 1990 national championship. Robert Joseph "Bobby" Ross' first season at Tech – 1987 – wasn't an indication of the greatness to come, with its meager 2-9 record. But the team improved steadily under his guidance, and from 1989-91, he led the Yellow Jackets to three consecutive seven-win seasons for the first time in nearly 30 years, as well as consecutive bowl berths in 1990-91 for the first time in 20 years. After struggling through a 5-20 mark in his first 25 games on the Flats, Ross teams then won 18 of their next 20 games.

In 1990, Ross directed Tech to the United Press International national championship as the nation's only unbeaten team at 11-0-1 following a convincing win over Nebraska in the Florida Citrus Bowl. The Jackets won the first Atlantic Coast Conference title in school history and their first national and conference championship of any kind since 1952.

A consensus National Coach of the Year and the ACC Coach of the Year, Ross returned Tech to the glory days of Bobby Dodd as the No. 1 ranked team by UPI, The Sporting News and Scripps Howard.

Ross collected the biggest win of his coaching career in 1990 when the Jackets knocked off No. 1-ranked Virginia, 41-38, in a nationally televised thriller in Charlottesville. A two-touchdown underdog, Tech came back from deficits of 13-0 and 28-14 before kicking the winning field goal with seven seconds left for an historic victory that vaulted the Yellow Jackets into the national spotlight.

Tech capped the storybook season by making its first appearance in a New Year's Day bowl since 1966 with its trip to the Citrus Bowl, beating Nebraska 45-21.

In 1991 - his final year on the Flats - Ross guided the Jackets to an 8-5 mark and a victory in the Aloha Bowl, marking Tech's first back-to-back bowl berths since 1971-72 and its first consecutive bowl victories since 1955-56. Following the win over Stanford, Ross accepted the head coaching position of the San Diego Chargers, a team he later would lead to the Super Bowl.

Ross became only the eighth full-time head football coach in Tech history on Jan. 5, 1987, after a month as an assistant coach with the NFL's Buffalo Bills. Ross was Tech's first head football coach since John Heisman not to have been a former Tech assistant coach or player.

Ross had joined the Bills after five successful seasons at Maryland. His Terrapin teams were known for their explosive offenses that resulted in the unprecedented success.

Following the 1996 season, Ross left the Chargers to become the head coach of the Detroit Lions, a position he held until the middle of the 2000 season, when he resigned. The Lions, whom Ross led to the postseason in 1999, have not returned to the playoffs since Ross's departure.

As head coach at Army, Ross reportedly received $600,000 in annual salary, which was seen as evidence of Army's eagerness to right the program after the team's 0–13 record in 2003. During his three year term as Army head coach, Ross improved their record to 9-25, up from 4-32 over the three years before Ross's arrival. Ross retired from coaching in 2007

What They've Said: *"If all the coaches in the country could be pooled for a draft, any school would do well to look at Bobby Ross closely and carefully. He's the best. You're talking about someone who went to a school where you could not lie, cheat, or steal, and lettered in three sports. He served in the military and recruited and coached at very tough academic schools. He's an astute student of the game, and he knows how to win, as a player and a coach. There's nobody better."*

— John McKenna, former Georgia Tech assistant athletics director

BY THE NUMBERS
BOBBY ROSS' COACHING CAREER

- 1973-77 – The Citadel
- 1982-86 – Maryland
- 1987-91 – Georgia Tech
- 1992-96 – San Diego Chargers
- 1997-2000 – Detroit Lions
- 2004-06 – Army

LET'S DON'T FORGET:

W.A. Alexander. Head football coach at Georgia Tech from 1920-1944 compiling a record of 134-95-15 ... Led Tech to the 1928 co-National Championship; 1921 SIAA title; 1922, 1927-1928 Southern Conference crowns; and SEC titles in 1939, 1943 and 1944 ... Became the first coach to take a program to all four major bowls: defeated California (8-7) in infamous "Wrong Way Riegels" 1929 Rose Bowl; defeated Missouri (21-7) in the 1940 Orange Bowl; lost to Texas (14-7) in the 1943 Cotton Bowl; defeated Tulsa (20-8) in the 1944 Sugar Bowl; and lost to Tulsa (26-12) in the 1945 Orange Bowl.

Bill Fincher. Two-time All-American (1919-1920) and two-time All-Southern Conference (1917 & '20) selection at Georgia Tech ... Tech football letterman from 1916-20 ... Member of the Tech All-Time Team and the College Football Hall of Fame.

JOHN SALLEY

The first player in NBA history to win a championship title with three different teams, "Spider" Salley was one of the NBA's most quotable and colorful players, even earning the distinction of being named the Best Interview in the NBA by the Associated Press for three straight years.

Salley played his college ball at Georgia Tech from 1982-86, and his No. 22 jersey hangs from Alexander Memorial Coliseum's rafters. He still holds the school's record for shot blocking. Salley's four-year Tech career saw him connect on 59 percent of his shots and average 34 minutes, 13 points and six rebounds per game. He graduated with a degree in industrial management and a minor in marketing.

"Spider" (so named for his long arms and legs) played for the Detroit Pistons from 1986-92, and was part of the franchise's back-to-back world championship teams in 1989 and '90. Salley remains No. 4 on the Pistons all-time shot blocking list (709).

From there, Salley went south to the Miami Heat, from 1992-95. He remains that franchise's third all-time best shot blocker (233). When the NBA expanded in the mid 1990s, Salley played for the Toronto Raptors in 1995-96 for 25 games as an expansion draft pick. From February '96 until the end of the season, Salley won his third championship ring as a member of the Chicago Bulls, the same year the Bulls set an all-time record by winning 72 games and losing 10.

After a three-year hiatus from the game, Salley joined the Los Angeles Lakers in 1999-2000, where he won his fourth championship ring for his third NBA team. A recognized leader in the locker room, Salley was elected player representative for the NBA Player's Association when playing for Detroit, Miami and Toronto.

During his NBA career and after, Salley appeared in numerous TV shows and movies as he attempted to carve out an acting career. He was a frequently sought-after NBA analyst and commentator, and enjoyed close friendships with entertainers such as comedian Eddie Murphy.

 *"Before I get drunk, I just want to sit here and thank you for putting up with my s#%& for three years. You took it like a man and you learned. You were developed and molded into exactly what we needed. And without you ... doing what you do, we wouldn't be here."*

— Bill Laimbeer to Salley after the Detroit Pistons won their first world championship

BY THE NUMBERS

PROFESSIONAL TEAM(S)

- Detroit Pistons (1986–1992)
- Miami Heat (1992–1995)
- Toronto Raptors (1995–1996)
- Chicago Bulls (1996)
- Panathinaikos BC (1996)
- Los Angeles Lakers (1999–2000)

CAREER STATS

Points 5,228
Rebounds 3,356
Blocks 983

PEARL SANDOW

Beginning in 1934, Sandow attended every professional baseball game played in Atlanta, except one, for the next 55 years. In the process, she became one of the city's most beloved figures, earning a place as one of the most dedicated fans in baseball history and a legitimate Atlanta sports legend.

Sandow, a native of Canton, first supported the Atlanta Crackers, who played at Ponce de Leon Ballpark. In 1966, when the Crackers folded in the wake of major league sports' first pro franchise south of the Mason-Dixon Line, she transferred her loyalty to the Atlanta Braves. In all, she saw more than 1,850 Crackers games and attended 1,889 Braves games - every Braves home contest from 1966-89.

Baseball was a lifelong passion for Sandow, whose mother took her to games as an infant. She missed only one game in 1961 - her first in more than 20 years - when her mother had a stroke. Sandow did not miss another Atlanta baseball game until she broke both shoulders in an accident in 1990. From that point on, Sandow was unable to go to the stadium, following instead her Braves on television and radio.

Sandow, who worked for 33 years as a department head in the federal government's housing program, organized her life around baseball. During the season she left her job and headed straight to the ballpark. Working for a living, Sandow claimed, interfered with baseball. She rarely missed batting practice and for 21 consecutive years went to spring training. She also attended the World Series numerous times, and accumulated one of the most extensive collections of Atlanta baseball memorabilia to be found anywhere.

Players, fans, and even former Braves owner Bill Bartholomay thought Sandow brought the team good luck. She was usually the first fan to arrive for a game, sitting in seat 1, row 9, section 105, behind the home dugout. Everyone easily recognized Sandow by her shock of white hair stacked high in what she called a snow-cone style.

In 1975 the Braves rewarded Sandow with a lifetime pass, a watch, and a night in her honor at the stadium. On May 12, 2002, the Braves brought her to Turner Field for the first time to celebrate her 100th birthday, making her team captain for the day. In 2005, she celebrated her 103rd birthday. She died in 2006.

Sandow's highest recognition came in 1989 when the National Baseball Hall of Fame in Cooperstown, New York, enshrined her in its fans section. There a statue honors Sandow's devotion to America's most popular pastime.

LET'S DON'T FORGET:

Joe Gerson. Born in Atlanta ... Co-founder and first president of the Atlanta Braves 400 Club ... Captain and four-year Georgia baseball letterman ... All-State baseball player at Boys' High ... One-time owner of the one of the state's most extensive collection of sports memorabilia.

JOHN SCHUERHOLZ

A sure-fire future Hall of Famer, Schuerholz oversaw the front-office and on-the-field transformation of a one-time woebegone baseball team into a symbol of professional sports excellence.

Before coming to the Atlanta Braves as general manager in late 1990, Schuerholz was general manager of the Kansas City Royals, where his stewardship resulted in a 1985 World Series championship. Schuerholz helped build the Royals into baseball's model expansion club throughout the '70s while serving in player development.

In Atlanta, Schuerholz's Braves won more games over a 15-year period than any other team in baseball, and won 14 consecutive division titles, a record unmatched by any other professional sports franchise in any other sport. No other modern professional sports executive has presided over such continued success.

Schuerholz continuously kept the Braves winning by swinging big trades (Fred McGriff, Gary Sheffield) and small (Otis Nixon); scouring both independent leagues (Kerry Ligtenberg) and the free-agent market (Terry Pendleton, Andres Galarraga); developing and folding in top prospects (Chipper Jones, Andruw Jones, Rafael Furcal), and all the while maintaining his pitching core (John Smoltz, Greg Maddux, Tom Glavine, Tim Hudson, and others).

When the Braves payroll was reduced after the 2001 season, critics suggested the team's dominance would finally come to an end. After all, other teams with large payrolls quickly disintegrated once the cash flow was reduced. But through astute financial management, shrewd free-agent scouting and an unparalleled farm system, Schuerholz kept the Braves on top despite injuries, free-agent departures and competition from other teams.

In 1966, Schuerholz was teaching junior high when he wrote a letter to his hometown Baltimore Orioles, asking for a job – any job – in baseball. He became an assistant to Lou Gorman, head of the team's farm system. Schuerholz followed Gorman to the expansion Kansas City Royals in 1968, where he was promoted from assistant farm director to farm director to director of player personnel, presiding over a minor-league system that produced the likes of George Brett, Dennis Leonard, Bret Saberhagen and Bo Jackson, constantly feeding teams that finished first or second every year from 1975-85.

Schuerholz has been the only general manager to build champions in both leagues. Immediately after his arrival in Atlanta, Schuerholz also began making moves that re-energized the fan base. After years of neglect and mismanagement, Atlanta-Fulton County was refurbished; top-notch groundskeeping personnel were hired; and concessions were diversified. Schuerholz knew how to build a winner both on and off the field, and the Braves completed an historic worst-to-first turnaround in 1991 that remains legendary in the annals of professional baseball.

In 2007, Schuerholz relinquished the reins as GM and handed them over to his protégé, Frank Wren. He retains the title of president of the Atlanta Braves. He was inducted into the Atlanta Sports Hall of Fame in 2008.

"In the highly competitive world of major league baseball, being able to win year after year is the mark of true leadership, skill, and talent. John Schuerholz is one of the very few who does precisely that – he wins, year after year."

— Rick Wolff, executive editor, vice president of Warner Books

TIM SIMPSON

Considered one of the best ball-strikers to ever play the game, Simpson was a four-time winner on the PGA Tour with more than $3.4 million in career winnings.

Born on May 6, 1956 in Atlanta, Simpson was a champion high school golfer at Woodward Academy. Among his many junior titles were the Atlanta PGA Championship; Georgia PGA Championship; and West Lake National Junior title.

Simpson's collegiate career at the University of Georgia included a two-time, First-Team All-SEC selection; a 1976 Third-Team All-American and honorable mention in 1975; and twice being named a member of the College All-Star team. He tied for 21st at the 1975 NCAA Championships, and 14th in '76. He also claimed medalist honors at the 1975 Palmetto.

Simpson turned pro on Christmas Day 1976. In 1981, '84 and '87, he won the Georgia Open Championship. Also in '81, he won the prestigious Cacheral World Championship in Nimes, France.

Simpson's first PGA victory came at the 1985 Southern Open in Georgia. He set the then PGA all-time record for hitting greens in regulation with 74 percent in 1989. He was also the first golfer to shoot 9-under after 36 holes in U.S. Open History. While winning his second 1990 Walt Disney Championship (the first came in 1989), he held the record for the lowest 54-hole total in PGA history (22-under).

Simpson defeated "the Shark," Greg Norman, to win the 1989 USF&G New Orleans Open. He played in the Sun City Million Dollar Challenge in South Africa - where only the 10 ten players in the world are invited – and finished third. He posted 11 top 10 finishes for 1989 season, and bettered that mark in 1990 with 12 top 10 placements.

Simpson's professional career was cut short when he contracted Lymes Disease.

LET'S DON'T FORGET:

Charles Harrison. Born in Atlanta ... Captured the 1955 Southern Amateur championship ... 1959 Georgia State Amateur champion ... 1955 Southern Amateur champion ... 1965 U.S. Open qualifier ... Ranked as the 13th-best amateur in America in 1966 ... First alternate on the U.S. Walker Cup team in '67 ... Quarterfinalist in the 1980 British Amateur ... Four-year golf letterman at Georgia Tech ... Captured the Atlanta City Amateur and the Atlanta Athletic Club titles nine times each and the Atlanta Country Club Championship six times ... Twice a member of the state of Georgia team that won the Bobby Jones trophy for the Southern States 4-Ball Championship ... Won the 1945 Atlanta Athletic Club Junior Championship, the '47 Atlanta City Junior Championship, and qualified for the '48 National Junior Championship ... President of the Atlanta Golf Association from 1971-85 ... Member of the Georgia Tech and Georgia Golf halls of fame.

MILDRED MCDANIEL SINGLETON

One of the top female athletes of the 1950s, Singleton excelled both in track and field and basketball. She set a world record in the high jump at 5'9 1/4" in the 1956 Olympic Games, and became the only U.S. woman to win a gold medal in track and field during those games as well.

Born Nov. 3, 1933, in Atlanta, Singleton was the youngest of three children. She was a reluctant athlete who became interested in basketball and the high jump by accident. She began playing basketball only after her gym teacher at Atlanta's David T. Howard High School offered any girl who made 10 consecutive free throws a new pair of shoes and a place on the team. McDaniel got the shoes.

McDaniel found she loved basketball, often earning high scorer honors. In the off-season most basketball players competed in track and field, but she was uninterested. The school's track coach, Marian Armstrong-Perkins - who had already sent three athletes to the Olympics - persuaded her to come watch track practice. While observing a girl practice the high jump, McDaniel commented to herself that the girl could not jump. Armstrong-Perkins overheard McDaniel and challenged her to jump. She was soon hooked and added hurdles, the broad jump, and the relay team to her repertoire. Besides capturing two state championships in basketball, McDaniel won state titles in the 80-yard hurdles, the high jump, and the long jump.

Singleton acquired her nickname of "Tex" on the basketball floor because her teammates said she dribbled like a Texan. A 1957 graduate of Tuskegee Institute in Alabama - where she was coached by Hall of Fame coach Cleve Abbott - she was the U.S. women's high jump champion in 1953, '55 and '56, and was the U.S. indoor champion the latter two years. She also was the 1955 Pan American Games winner with a leap of 5-6 1/4, a meet mark which stood until 1967.

In 1957 McDaniel graduated with a degree in physical education, was named Woman of the Year (Atlanta), won the AAU's Sullivan Award for sportsmanship, and had her picture on a postage stamp in the Dominican Republic.

RANKIN SMITH, SR.

Were it not for a young, little-known insurance agent who was at the forefront of Atlanta history in the 1960s, the city might never have landed a professional football team.

But on June 30, 1965, Smith paid a then-record $8.5 million to win the National Football League's 23rd professional football franchise and the first in the Deep South. Over the next 30 some-odd years, the Atlanta Falcons would achieve varying levels of success on the field and the owner himself became the butt of jokes and criticism, but the fact remains that without Smith, Atlanta would not be enjoying the electrifying athleticism of Matt Ryan and Co., nor be the home of the world's premier indoor sporting venues, the Georgia Dome.

Virtually unknown to the general public before that June day, Smith immediately endeared himself to aficionados of the sport by asking a rhetorical question at a press conference following his securing of the franchise: "Doesn't every adult male in America want to own his own football team?"

By the time Smith got back to his insurance office 24 hours after writing the check, there had been more than 1,000 phone calls for tickets. He had to push his way through stacks of mail. By August, a name-the-team contest was completed. Several persons suggested the name "Falcons" in a contest, but a school teacher from nearby Griffin, Julia Elliott, was selected winner because of her reasons: "The falcon is proud and dignified, with great courage and fight. It never drops prey. It is deadly and has a great sporting tradition."

Smith signed the nation's most coveted college football player, Texas linebacker Tommy Nobis. By Christmas Eve, when the Falcons cut off a brief 54-day ticket sale requiring almost no promotion, an NFL record had been established for season tickets sold by a new club (45,000).

In the 1990s, Smith began lobbying for the construction of the Georgia Dome, and played a role in securing the 1994 Super Bowl to be played in the new facility. He also served on NFL expansion committees that helped bring teams to Jacksonville and Charlotte, N.C. And in 1985 he began the Falcons Youth Foundation in 1985 that has aided hundreds of city, county and state charities.

Smith endured much criticism over the years for his stewardship of the Falcons, as the franchise to this day has never posted consecutive winning seasons. Nonetheless, the team did play in its one and only Super Bowl in 1998, an accomplishment Smith did not live to see.

What They've Said: *"There were constants in his life: family, the city of Atlanta, the South and the NFL. He made some outstanding contributions to this city (Atlanta) and was a supporter of non-profit organizations around the state."*

— Tommy Nobis

LET'S DON'T FORGET:

Thomas J. Slate ... Atlanta native and longtime football official who helped inaugurate the University of Georgia-Georgia Tech Scottish Rite Freshman Football Classic.

George Crumbley. Founder of a little-known college football bowl game in the 1960s that became the modern-day, multi-million-dollar payout Chick-fil-A Bowl ... Kept the contest going against all odds, including a poor football facility in Atlanta-Fulton County Stadium and continual inclement weather that occurred annually on game day.

ROBERT WILLIAM "RED" SMITH

One of the most successful track coaches in the nation, Smith formed the Northside Red Runners in 1971 with five female runners. From that humble beginning, the program has grown to the point where Smith produced 600 county champions, 300 state champions, 50 national champions, and 10 national cross country champions.

Smith's program encouraged female athletes pursuing track and field and cross-country opportunities to excel in high school and college programs. More than 25 percent of his athletes were awarded scholarships to colleges across the United States and 32 were participants in the opening and closing ceremonies at the 1996 Olympic Games.

Smith was an excellent athlete in his own right. At Atlanta Boys' High School, he captained and coached the track and cross country teams. He won the state cross country championship two consecutive years, and was named to the cross country and track and field all-state teams.

Smith won an athletic scholarship to Georgia Tech where he was twice captain of the cross country team and once co-captain of the track team. He won the Southeastern Conference cross country title his junior year when he set a Tech school record of 18 minutes and 42 seconds for four miles on the old Howell Mill course.

After graduating from Georgia Tech, Red was commissioned a 2nd lieutenant in the U.S. Army. After two years of active duty - one in combat in Korea - and 18 in the Reserve, he retired as a lieutenant colonel. He spent more than 40 years in insurance sales at Pacific Mutual and volunteered almost all the rest of his waking hours to young athletes, molding them into track and cross-country champions.

As a result of Smith's leadership, about 4,000 kids have gone through the program over the years, and several still have national records in the Junior Olympics. Smith himself coached more than 3,000 runners, including sisters Andrea and Tenisha King. The former was a five-time NCAA All-American and a five-time Atlantic Coast Conference women's indoor and outdoor MVP at Georgia Tech, and won the 100-meter hurdles at the 1999 World University Games. Her sister won a track scholarship to Notre Dame where she won a 100-meters hurdles championship at the Missouri Invitational.

Smith died in 2008 from complications from Parkinson's Disease.

LET'S DON'T FORGET:

Jimmy Carnes. 1980 United States Olympic Track & Field head coach ... Track coach at Atlanta's Druid Hills High School from 1956-1962, Furman University (1962-1964) and the University of Florida (1964-1976) ... Posted a 161-11 record during 20 years of coaching track and field ... Compiled a 52-0 record with 27 championships and six state crowns at Druid Hills ... Two track teams at Furman were 16-3 in dual meeting and won both the Southern Conference Indoor and Outdoor titles ... Captured two SEC Indoor championships with a 93-3 mark at the University of Florida ... Georgia Coach of the Year six times.

MAE LOUISE SUGGS

The first woman inducted in the LPGA Hall of Fame, Suggs captured 50 tour titles throughout her career and was named to *Golf Magazine's* "100 Heroes" during the 1988 Centennial of Golf in America celebration.

Born in Atlanta, Suggs had a brilliant amateur career. She won the Georgia State Amateur Championship in 1940 and '42, captured the Southern Amateur Championship in '41 and '47; and was a three-time winner of the North/South Championship (1942, '46, and '48). Suggs won the 1946 Western Amateur Championship and Western Open and successfully defended both titles the following season. She won the Titleholders in 1946, and in '47 became the U.S. Women's Amateur champion. Suggs added the British Amateur Championship to her resume and topped off her amateur career by representing the United States on the 1948 Curtis Cup Team.

Suggs turned professional in 1948, and of her 50 tour titles, eight were majors: 1949 and '52 U.S. Women's Open; 1954, '56 and '59 Titleholders; 1949 and '53 Western Open; and the 1957 LPGA Championship.

Suggs was a founder and charter member of the LPGA. She was the first LPGA player to win a tournament for three consecutive years: the Dallas Civitan Open from 1959-61. Her 1949 U.S. Women's Open victory was a 14-stroke victory that set a 72-hole scoring record of 291. That contest also set an all-time record for margin of victory that was not equaled until 1986 when Cindy Mackey did so at the MasterCard International.

In 1953, Suggs broke her own 72-hole scoring record by shooting 288 to win the Tampa Open.

Suggs was the winner of the 1957 Vare Trophy. During a practice round for the 1991 Centel Senior Challenge, she recorded her first career hole-in-one.

Nicknamed "Miss Sluggs" by legendary entertainer Bob Hope, Suggs served as LPGA president three times and was named an Honorary Member of the LPGA Teaching and Club Professionals Division in 1993. The 1995 LPGA Championship was dedicated in her honor. In 1996 she was the first woman elected to the Georgia Athletic Hall of Fame, and, in 2007, she was inducted into the Atlanta Sports Hall of Fame.

(Continued on next page)

MAE LOUISE SUGGS

 *"Honesty is the biggest part of golf. I believe people who cheat on the golf course will cheat anywhere. Golf is true to life. Live it the right way and you'll be OK."*
— Louise Suggs

BY THE NUMBERS

MAJOR VICTORIES

1949: U.S. Women's Open, Western Open

1951: U.S. Women's Open

1953: Western Open

1954: Titleholders Championship

1956: Titleholders Championship

1957: LPGA Championship

1959: Titleholders Championship

LPGA TOUR VICTORIES

1949: All-American Open

1951: Carrollton Open

1952: Jacksonville Open, Tampa Open, Stockton Open, All-American Open, Betty Jameson Open

1953: Tampa Open, Betsy Rawls Open, San Diego Open, San Francisco Weathervane, Bakersfield Open, Philadelphia Weathervane Open, Cross Country Weathervane

1954: Sea Island Open, Betsy Rawls Open, Carrollton Open, Babe Zaharias Open

1955: Los Angeles Open, Oklahoma City Open, Eastern Open, Triangle Round Robin, St. Louis Open

1956: Havana Open, All-American Open

1957: Heart of America Invitational

1958: Babe Zaharias Open, Gatlinburg Open, French Lick Open, Triangle Round Robin

1959: St. Petersburg Open, Dallas Civitan Open

1960: Dallas Civitan Open, Triangle Round Robin, Youngstown Kitchens Open, San Antonio Civitan Open

1961: Royal Poinciana Invitational, Golden Circle of Golf, Dallas Civitan Open, Kansas City Open, San Antonio Civitan

1962: St. Petersburg Open

GWEN TORRENCE

At one time one of the fastest women in the world, Atlanta native Gwen Torrence captured gold medals in the 400-meter relay and 200-meter dash at the 1992 Barcelona Olympic Games; and a third gold in the 400-meter relay at the 1996 Atlanta Olympic Games. Considered by many to be one of the sprinters to ever set foot on a track, Torrence also garnered a silver medal in the 1,600-meter relay in 1992 and a bronze in the 100 meters in 1996.

The youngest of five children, Torrence was born with her umbilical cord around her neck. She suffered no ill effects from her precarious start in life, and her running ability first attracted attention when she was a Columbia High School student in DeKalb County. Her physical education teacher noticed her speed and timed Torrence in the 220-yard dash. She broke the state record wearing street clothes and low-heeled shoes.

Torrence won three consecutive state 100- and 200-meter dash championships, earning All-American honors her senior year, 1982-83. That summer she also won two gold medals at the Junior Olympics. The University of Georgia then offered Torrence a full scholarship, and she became the first in her family to attend college.

During her years at UGA, Torrence earned All-American honors 12 times and won four NCAA championship titles. During her freshman season (1983-84) she received an invitation to the U.S. Olympic Trials, but declined because she felt that she was too young.

Torrence improved every year, winning at the 1986 Millrose Games, held at Madison Square Garden, and the 1987 World University Games, held in Zagreb, Yugoslavia. She also proved herself in the classroom, graduating in 1987 with a degree in early childhood education.

At the 1988 Millrose Games, again held at Madison Square Garden, Torrence won her 33rd consecutive race and became the woman to beat in the Seoul Olympics. Florence Griffith-Joyner, however, shocked the world by beating Torrence and setting new world records for both the 100- and 200-meter dash.

Torrence soon set her sights on the 1992 Olympics in Barcelona. She lost the 100-meter to Gail Devers but won a gold medal in the 200-meter. She won gold for her participation in the 400-meter relay team and a silver for running on the 1600-meter relay team. She also won gold for the 100-meter at the World Championship Games in Gothenberg, Sweden.

LET'S DON'T FORGET:

Mel Pender. Born in Atlanta ... Member of the United States' gold medal winning 400-meter relay team at the 1968 Mexico City Olympic Games in a world record time of 38.2 ... Captured his gold medal at the age of 31 ... Became the only U.S. sprinter to qualify for and run in both the 1964 Tokyo and 1968 Olympic Games placing sixth in the 100 meters each of these years ... Narrowly missed qualifying for a third Olympic appearance at age 35 by two-one-hundreths of a second ... As a commanding officer in the 82nd Airborne, he earned a Bronze Star for his service in Vietnam and also served as the U.S. Military Academy's head track coach.

JESSIE TUGGLE

After joining Atlanta as an undrafted rookie free agent out of Valdosta State in 1987, "The Hammer" went on to play 13 years with the Falcons, earning a reputation as one of the hardest-hitting and best-conditioned linebackers of his time.

A player whose self-professed goal was to simply play hard on each and every single down regardless of the score (which, too often, was stacked against the Falcons), Tuggle's total of 2,065 career tackles is the most in team history. Along the way, he earned five Pro Bowl appearances and led the Falcons in tackles in 10 of his 14 seasons, including a stretch of 12-straight 100-tackle seasons. He also led the NFL in tackles with 201 in 1990 and 207 the following year. Tuggle also holds the NFL record for most touchdowns by recovery of opponents' fumbles with five.

Tuggle helped guide the Falcons to the NFC Championship and Super Bowl XXXIII for the first time in franchise history in 1998. He also holds the franchise playoff record for most tackles in a game with 11 in the NFC Championship Game vs. Minnesota.

Tuggle played his entire career in the state of Georgia from high school (Griffin) and college (Valdosta State) to the professional ranks (Atlanta Falcons). He left as Valdosta State's all-time record holder with 340 tackles, and a senior, he was the Gulf South Conference Defensive Player of the Year. His No. 88 jersey was retired by the school in 1993.

Tuggle's No. 57 jersey was retired by the Atlanta Falcons in its inaugural Ring of Honor ceremony.

LET'S DON'T FORGET:

Larry Morris. Born in Decatur, GA ... Two-time first-team football All-American in 1952 and '53 (consensus) ... All-SEC four straight years ... 1954 SEC Lineman of the Year by the Atlanta Touchdown Club ... Four-year starter for the Rambling Wreck as a linebacker and center from 1951-54 ... Selected to the Quarter Century All-SEC Team (1950-74) ... Played 11 seasons in the NFL for the Los Angeles Rams, Chicago Bears and the Atlanta Falcons ... MVP in the Bears' world championship victory over the New York Giants.

Clarence Scott. Born in Decatur, GA ... The No. 1 draft choice of the Cleveland Browns in 1971 ... Played his entire career with the Browns from 1971-83 ... A first-team All-Pro selection and Pro Bowl participant in 1974 ... Intercepted 39 passes and returned two for touchdowns during NFL career ... Terrorized Pro Football Hall of Fame quarterback Terry Bradshaw by intercepting him six times during his career ... Member of the 1965 Class A State Championship Decatur High team.

Patrick Swilling. Five-time NFL Pro Bowl selection during his 12-year professional career ... A stellar defensive end earning the 1989 NFL Defensive Player of the Year award for the New Orleans Saints ... Collected 107.5 sacks that ranks in the top 20 in NFL history ... Professional career: New Orleans Saints, 1986-92; Detroit Lions, 1993-94; Oakland Raiders, 1995-97) ... Collegiate career: Georgia Tech, 1982-85) ... One of the main players in Tech's gridiron resurgence ... 1985 First-Team All-American and All ACC pick ... Set single season Yellow Jacket record with 15 sacks for minus 119 yards... Still holds the ACC single game sack mark with seven against N.C. State in 1985 ... Finished collegiate career as Tech's leader in sacks (23) and tackles for loss (37).

R.E. "TED" TURNER

The man who made the Atlanta Braves the real "America's Team" is one of the nation's true renaissance men, with interests ranging from ecology and conservation to true and lasting global peace. But when Turner began his broadcasting empire with a low-frequency UHF channel in the 1970s, no one could have imagined he would become one of the world's most recognizable figures.

Born in Cincinnati, Ohio, Turner's family moved to Savannah when he was nine years old. He attended the McCallie School in Chattanooga, TN, and received a degree from Brown University, where he was vice president of the Debating Union and commodore of the Yacht Club.

In 1963, Turner became president and COO of Turner Advertising, a company whose profits he used to help purchase a failing Atlanta UHF station, WJRJ, in 1968. He immediately renamed the station WTCG (for Turner Communications Group) and began to look for programming. What Turner found were old movies and syndicated television series, many of which he purchased outright with a view toward unrestricted future showings. He used these to counter-program the network affiliates, going after such audience segments as children and people who did not watch the news.

By the early 1970s, WTBS (formerly known as WTCG) also offered local sports programming - first professional wrestling and then Atlanta Braves baseball, Atlanta Hawks basketball, and Atlanta Flames hockey. In 1976, Turner purchased the Braves, securing long-term access to his single most critical source of programming. The team became Turner's broadcasting mainstay, and in 1977, Turner bought the Atlanta Hawks. The same year, he won the America's Cup, yachting's most prestigious event, as captain of the boat "Courageous." Over the years, Turner would also win the 1979 Fastnet Trophy and four Yachtsman of the Year awards.

Turner gained a reputation as one of the nation's most outspoken, colorful millionaires (soon to be, billionaires). While his Braves fielded mostly unsuccessful teams, Turner himself was always willing to try new approaches to boost attendance and interest (he even named himself manager of the team for one game!)

As 1980 dawned, Turner emerged as a true broadcast visionary, pioneering the notion of TV "super-station" broadcasting to cable systems nationwide by means of satellite. CNN was launched in 1980, the world's first, live, in-depth, round-the-clock news television network. A second all-news service, Headline News, began operation on January 1, 1982. CNN International was launched in 1985, the same year that Turner originated the Goodwill Games as an international, world-class, quadrennial, multi-sport competition. The inaugural Games were held in July 1986 in Moscow and were followed by the 1990 Games in Seattle, WA; the 1994 Games in St. Petersburg, Russia; the 1998 Games in New York City; the first winter games in Lake Placid, NY, in 2000; and the last of the Goodwill Games in Brisbane, Australia, in 2001.

(Continued on next page)

R.E. "TED" TURNER

Turner won his one and only baseball world championship in 1995, when the Braves defeated the Cleveland Indians in six games. Following the merger of Turner Broadcasting and Time Warner, he became vice chairman of the new parent company in October 1996. Time Warner eventually became the owners of the Braves, Hawks, and the city's second NHL franchise, the Thrashers. (When Atlanta was awarded the franchise, Turner was asked what he thought would be a good moniker for the team. The company was under no obligation to choose his suggestion, but did so nonetheless, a testament to Turner's influence.)

Turner also renewed his professional wrestling programming in the late 1990s, making his World Championship Wrestling organization a major marketing and merchandising entity.

When the Braves moved into Atlanta's former Olympic Stadium in 1997, which had been converted to one of Major League's Baseball's premier coliseums, the franchise christened their new home Turner Field, another nod to Turner's legacy as one of the city's legendary sports figures.

"All my life people have said I wasn't going to make it."
— Ted Turner

"I'm 80 years old, and Ted is 70. Over the next decade, I can't wait to see how he will continue to change our world."
— T. Boone Pickens, *TIME* Magazine

JEFF VAN NOTE

Playing in 246 games and starting 225 of those, Van Note is one of the longest-serving players not only in Atlanta Falcons history, but also the NFL.

Born Feb. 7, 1946 in South Orange, NJ, 'Note played his entire 18-year professional career with the Falcons. His 246 games played ranks in the top 25 in NFL history, right alongside some of the NFL's greatest like Fran Tarkenton, Nick Lowery, Mike Webster, Jackie Slater, Clay Matthews, and Earl Morrell.

'Note played in 155 consecutive games for Atlanta from 1976-86. The six-time Pro Bowler missed only four games in his NFL career. His No. 57 jersey was retired at halftime of his final home game, Dec. 15, 1986. Falcons' fans voted him as the franchise's favorite player during Atlanta's 25th season.

Van Note originally came to the Falcons as a linebacker out of the University of Kentucky, but was moved to center by then-head coach Norm Van Brocklin, and played in the Blue-Gray All-Star game before beginning his professional career.

'Note maintained his relationship with the club after his retirement as the team's lead color analyst for its radio broadcasts. He also has covered the Tennessee Titans, Kentucky football, the Southeastern Conference Championship Game, the Peach Bowl and Southern Conference football. He also worked the talk-show circuit on WSB radio alongside the legendary Larry Munson, and spent a few years in the booth with another well-known Atlanta radio voice, Wes Durham, familiar to Georgia Tech fans as the voice of the Yellow Jackets.

Van Note is a member of the Atlanta Falcons' Ring of Honor, and he was inducted into the Atlanta Sports Hall of Fame in 2007.

LET'S DON'T FORGET:

Mike Kenn. Offensive lineman for the Atlanta Falcons for 17 years ... The team's No. 1 draft pick in 1978 ... Gained a reputation as one of the league's most technically proficient blockers ... Went more than a dozen seasons without being flagged for an offensive blocking penalty ... Went on to enjoy a successful and influential career in local politics ... Member of the All-Time Atlanta Falcons team ... Inducted into the 2008 Atlanta Falcons Ring of Honor.

William L. "Billy" Shaw. Member of the Georgia Tech Hall of Fame ... Selected as the SEC's Most Outstanding Offensive Lineman in 1960 by the Birmingham Monday Morning Quarterback Club ... 1960 All-SEC 1st-team pick by Associated Press and United Press International ... Made the 1957 All-SEC Freshman team ... Chosen to the All-Time Bobby Dodd team (1945-66) at offensive guard ... 1999 inductee into the Pro Football Hall of Fame...Played for the Buffalo Bills from 1961-69...Named to pro football's All-Decade Team of the 1960s, the All-Time AFL Team, and first-team All-AFL from 1962-66 ... Helped lead the Bills to the 1964 and '65 AFL Championships.

JASON VARITEK

The only baseball player to ever have his number (33) retired by Georgia Tech, Varitek earned a reputation for being one of the best that the Major Leagues has to offer.

Primarily a third baseman while playing high school ball in Longwood, FL, Varitek is one of only two players in baseball history to have completed in the Little League World Series (1984); the national championship game of the College World Series (1994); and the World Series (2004 and 2007). He's the only player to have appeared in all three of those series and represent the United States in the Olympics (1992) and the World Baseball Classic (2006). The three-time All-American was named Baseball America's College Player of the Year in 1993; later, the publication named him to its "All-Time College All-Star Team."

Varitek joined fellow Atlanta Sports Legends Nomar Garciaparra and Kevin Brown as one of three baseball players among Georgia Tech's 50 Greatest Athletes of the 20th Century. Varitek was drafted by the Minnesota Twins in the first round (21st overall) in 1993, but opted to return to school. The following year, he was drafted by the Seattle Mariners with the 14th overall selection. Along with Derek Lowe, Varietek was shipped to the Boston Red Sox in 1997.

In 2003, Varitek made his first All-Star team when he hit .273 with 25 homers and 85 RBI. He was ninth in the league with 39 doubles. While in Boston, Varitek was a career .265 hitter with 79 homers and 345 RBI in seven seasons.

In 2004, Varitek was one of the Red Sox's leaders that led the franchise to its first world championship in more than 80 years. He appeared in every game and started 13 of 14 post-season contests behind the plate, and hit .245 (13-for-53) in the post-season with three homers and 11 RBI.

In 2005, the captain of the Red Sox had another solid season on both sides of the ball, making his first start in an All-Star Game. Even though the Red Sox made an early exit from the playoffs, Varitek led his team with 4.15 pitches per plate appearance, and batted .320.

In 2007, Varitek and the Red Sox returned to the World Series once again, winning for the second time in four years. During the season, Varitek enjoyed a couple of personal highlights, reaching his 1000th career hit. On May 19, 2008, he caught Jon Lester's no-hitter, giving him a Major League record of having caught four separate no-hitters in his career.

During the 2008 offseason, he signed a four-year, $40 million contract with the Red Sox.

LET'S DON'T FORGET:

Virlyn Moore, Jr. Born in Atlanta ... Played catcher on the United States 1936 Berlin Olympic Games baseball team ... Also played catcher on Georgia's 1933 SEC Championship baseball team ... Led Georgia's 1933 basketball team in scoring-the only year which he played ... Former president of the Atlanta Tip Off Club.

LEONARD RANDOLPH WILKENS

After a Hall of Fame career as one of the great playmakers in basketball history, Wilkens turned to coaching and led his teams to more wins than any other coach in NBA history. And one of those teams was a franchise not often associated with success, the Atlanta Hawks.

Wilkens signed on to coach the Atlanta Hawks for the 1993-94 season, and his team-oriented strategy quickly began to work. The Hawks, who had finished 43-39 the previous season, set a team record for scoring defense (96.2 points allowed per game). They finished the campaign at 57-25, matching the best record in franchise history and winning their first Central Division title since 1987.

In 1994-95, the Hawks recovered from a sluggish start to go 42-40 and earn a spot in the playoffs, where they were eliminated by Indiana. They improved by four wins in 1995-96, and stunned favored Indiana in the first round of the playoffs before bowing to Orlando led by Shaquille O'Neal in the conference semifinals. And they continued to build in Wilkens' defensive mold by signing free agent center Dikembe Mutombo, the NBA's shotblocking king, in the summer of 1996.

For Wilkens, however, the summer of 1996 will be remembered for the time spent coaching the Dream Team to Olympic gold. Despite some slow starts and close first half play, Team USA won each of its games by at least 18 points and defeated Yugoslavia 95-69 in the gold medal game.

The Hawks improved by 10 games to 56-26 in 1996-97 to finish second behind Chicago in the Central Division. Atlanta then defeated Detroit 3-2 in a spirited first round playoff series before losing to the eventual champion Bulls in five games in the Eastern Conference Semifinals. In 1998 Wilkens was enshrined a second time – this time, as a coach – in the NBA Hall of Fame.

On Jan. 6, 1995, in his 22nd NBA season as a head coach, Wilkens became the winningest coach in NBA history, notching his 939th coaching victory to surpass Boston Celtics legend Red Auerbach's 938. The milestone victory came when Wilkens and the Hawks defeated Washington 112-90 at the Omni in Atlanta, with Auerbach on hand.

Wilkens reached another milestone on March 1, 1996, when his Hawks defeated the Cleveland Cavaliers 74-68, making him the first coach in NBA history to record 1,000 regular season NBA victories.

Wilkens' career in basketball almost foundered at the start. Despite making the Boys High School team in Brooklyn, N.Y. as a freshman (the last man on a 12-man squad), Wilkens did not go out for the team the next two years because he didn't think he was good enough to play. He honed his skills instead in various Catholic Youth Organization leagues.

During Wilkens' 15 years as a player in the NBA, he scored 17,772 points for an average of 16.5 ppg and handed out 7,211 assists. He ranks among the all-time leaders in assists, games played, minutes played and free throws made.

BY THE NUMBERS

AWARDS

- Nine-time All-Star
- All-Star Game MVP (1972)
- NBA's 50th Anniversary All-Time Team
- NBA Hall of Fame, class of 1989 (as player)
- NBA Hall of Fame, class of 1998 (as coach)

JACQUES DOMINIQUE WILKINS

One of the NBA's true marquee players for more than a decade, Wilkins earned the nickname "human highlight film" with a plethora of spectacular individual plays dating back to his college years at Georgia. A member of the NBA All-Rookie Team in 1983, the high-flying 6-8 forward was named to seven All-NBA teams and nine consecutive All-Star squads and is a two-time winner of the NBA Slam-Dunk Championship.

Born in Paris, France, where his father was stationed in the U.S. Air Force, Wilkins attended high school in Washington, N.C. The older brother of NBA player Gerald Wilkins, Dominique attended college at the University of Georgia, where he averaged 21.6 points over three seasons. It was there that his acrobatic exploits earned him the famous moniker.

Wilkins entered the 1982 NBA draft after his junior year and was selected by the Utah Jazz with the third overall pick. He refused to sign with the Jazz, however, and was dealt in September 1982 to the Atlanta Hawks for John Drew, Freeman Williams and cash.

Wilkins was an instant hit for the Hawks, averaging 17.5 points per game as a rookie. He came back in his second season with an average of 21.6 points per game, starting a remarkable streak in which he would average above 20 points per contest for 11 consecutive seasons.

Wilkins was instrumental to the Hawks' success in the late 1980s as the club recorded 50 wins in four straight seasons from 1985-86 to 1988-89. During that span he poured in more than 30 points per game twice, and for the four years combined he averaged 29.1 points per game. In 1986 he won the NBA scoring title with an average of 30.3 points per game, and in .92 he set an NBA record by sinking 23 free throws in a game without a miss (he remains the Atlanta Hawks' all-time franchise leader in both scoring and steals).

In 1988 Wilkins scored 29 points in 30 minutes of action in the All-Star Game. In the postseason he averaged 31.2 points and despite the Hawks narrowly missing out on reaching the Eastern Conference Finals after losing to the Boston Celtics by a mere two points in game seven of the conference semifinals, he gained more respect as a result of his epic battle with Larry Bird.

In the early '90s, while the Hawks were slipping from a 50-win team to a .500 ballclub, Wilkins evolved from a pure scorer into a more all-around contributor. In 1990-91 he grabbed a career-high nine rebounds per contest, and he topped three assists per game that year for the first time.

Nearly injury-free for most of his career, Wilkins suffered a season-ending rupture of his Achilles tendon midway through the 1991-92 campaign. Some thought the injury might end Wilkins's career, but the 32-year-old bounced back in grand fashion the next year, averaging 29.9 points per game to finish second to NBA legend Michael Jordan for the league scoring crown while maintaining his solid all-around play. That same season he became the 17th player in NBA history to rack up 20,000 points.

Midway through the 1993-94 season - Wilkins' 12th with Atlanta - the Hawks shocked their fans by trading their all-time leading scorer to the Los Angeles Clippers for Danny Manning. Wilkins became a free agent after the season and signed with the Boston Celtics for 1994-95. Although he was the Celtics' leading scorer, his average of 17.8 points per game was his lowest mark since his rookie season.

The summer following the season, Wilkins, unhappy with his role on the rebuilding Celtics, signed to play for Panathinaikos Athens of the Greek League. He averaged 20.9 points and seven rebounds in 14 games for Panathinaikos and led the team to the European Championship for Men's Clubs in 1996. Wilkins was named the MVP of the European Final Four in Paris.

Before the 1996-97 season, Wilkins returned to the NBA, signing a contract as a free agent with the San Antonio Spurs, who were seeking to add bench scoring. Wilkins gave them more than they could have hoped for, leading the team with an average of 18.2 points per game in 1996-97 and also contributing 6.4 rebounds per game. However, after one season, Wilkins once again went overseas, this time signing a contract with Teamsystem in Italy for the 1997-98 season.

One season later, Wilkins returned for his last NBA campaign alongside his brother Gerald with the Orlando Magic. Wilkins left the NBA ranked seventh on the all-time scoring list with 26,534 points and 10th in career scoring average at 25.3 points per game.

When the Atlanta Hawks came under new ownership in 2004, they wisely placed Wilkins in a high profile and influential front office leadership position, thus ensuring that the human highlight film will always be associated with the franchise both on the court and off.

Wilkins was part of the original class of inductees in the Atlanta Sports Hall of Fame.

BY THE NUMBERS

CAREER HIGHLIGHTS AND AWARDS

- NBA All-Rookie Team (1983)
- 2-time NBA Slam Dunk Contest Champion (1985, 1990)
- 9-time NBA All Star (1986-94)
- NBA Scoring Champ 1986
- All-NBA First Team selection
- 4-time All-NBA Second Team selection
- 2-time All-NBA Third Team selection
- FIBA World Championship Gold Medal 1994
- Greek Cup Champion 1996
- Greek Cup MVP 1996
- Euroleague Champion 1996
- Euroleague Finals Most Valuable Player Award 1996

JOHN WHITLOW WYATT

Manager of one of the greatest teams to ever wear an Atlanta Cracker uniform. Wyatt and the franchise made history in 1954 by winning the midseason All-Star game; winning the league pennant; winning the postseason league playoffs; and finally winning the Dixie Series over the Texas League champions, thus winning the Southern Association grand slam a second time. No other team in league history accomplished the feat more than once.

Wyatt was one of the best pitchers in baseball, compiling a record of 78 wins and 39 losses from 1939-43. Named to the National League All-Star Team four, Wyatt struggled for the first nine years of his career, winning 26 games and losing 32. Three American League teams released him. After the 1937 season Wyatt retired from baseball and returned to his farm in Buchanan, GA.

The Milwaukee Brewers of the American Association persuaded Wyatt to give baseball one last try. There, he mastered the slow curve, an accomplishment that proved to be the turning point in his career. In 1938 he won the pitchers' triple crown, leading the association in wins, strikeouts, and earned run average. League writers named Wyatt MVP. After the season, the Brooklyn Dodgers bought his contract for $30,000, and he enjoyed five outstanding years in the major leagues.

Wyatt's best season was 1941, when he tied for the league lead in victories, with 22, and led the Dodgers to their first pennant since 1920. He won the second game of the World Series, ending the New York Yankees' streak of 10 consecutive victories in series play. He lost the final game of the series, but he struck out Joe DiMaggio twice, the only time that DiMaggio fanned twice in the same game all season.

From 1955-69 Wyatt was pitching coach for the Philadelphia Phillies as well as the Milwaukee and Atlanta Braves.

LET'S DON'T FORGET:

Eddie Mathews. Managed the 1972-74. Was the manager when Hank Aaron hit his 715th home run ... Regarded as one of the strongest power hitters of his time, often being compared to Mickey Mantle ... Made his professional debut in Atlanta in 1954 as a member of the Crackers ... Along with Aaron, helped lead the Milwaukee Braves to a 1957 World Series title.

RICH YUNKUS

Only the second player to ever have his jersey retired by Georgia Tech, Yunkus dominated the pivot position for the Yellow Jackets from 1968-70.

Yunkus was a first-team All-American in 1970 and 1971, and was Tech's all-time leading scorer with 2,232 points and a career average of 26.6 points per game. A three-time academic All-American, Yunkus' seasonal marks never dipped below 24 points and 11 rebounds per games. In 1971 the Yellow Jackets, led by Yunkus, reached the finals of the National Invitation Tournament but lost to the University of North Carolina.

What's even more remarkable about Yunkus' accomplishments is that freshmen weren't eligible under NCAA rules during his collegiate career. Fellow Atlanta Sports Legend Matt Harpring came closest to Yunkus, amassing 2,225 points. Harpring played from 1995-1998, one more season than Yunkus. Harpring played in 40 more games than Yunkus and hit 210 3-pointers. And the three-point shot didn't exist during Yunkus' 1969-1971 career.

Yunkus still ranks among the greatest in Tech history in numerous categories. He scored 40 or more points in a game six times; and 30 or more 19 times. He led Tech to the 1970 and 1971 National Invitational Tournament, and was drafted in 1971 by the NBA's Cincinnati Royals (third round) and the American Basketball Association's Carolina team.

He also is a member of the Georgia Tech Hall of Fame, as well as the Georgia Sports Hall of Fame.

One of Yunkus' career highlights was finishing runner-up to North Carolina in the National Invitation Tournament in New York City in 1971. In those days only 16 teams made the NCAA Tournament and only 16 were invited to the NIT. Southern Illinois University won the NIT in 1967 with another Atlanta Sports Legend, Walt Frazier.

After college, Yunkus played one-third of a season for the Atlanta Hawks with Atlanta Sports Legend Pete Maravich, but decided the pros weren't for him. The Hawks released Yunkus in 1972, and his family purchased a Terminex business that he ran with his father. They eventually sold the business in 1989, and Yunkus is currently a representative for Edward Jones in Benton, IL.

LET'S DON'T FORGET:

Donald "Duck" Priestly Stephenson. 1956 and '57 first-team All-American at center for Georgia Tech ... Voted first-team All-SEC in '56 and '57 ... Three-year starter helped lead Tech to consecutive bowl wins over Pittsburgh in the '56 Sugar Bowl (7-0) and the '56 Gator Bowl (21-14) ... Member of the Georgia Tech Hall of Fame ... Played nine years in teh Canadian Football League with Edmonmton and Calgary, and played both offense and defense wihile with Edmonton.

ATLANTA'S HISTORIC SPORTING VENUES

ALEXANDER MEMORIAL COLISEUM

Regarded as one of the toughest arenas for opposing teams in the Atlantic Coast Conference, the Alexander Memorial Coliseum at McDonald's Center on the Georgia Tech campus has been the home court for the Yellow Jackets for more than five decades.

Dubbed "The Thrillerdome" as a tribute to the many dramatic finishes to games there in the Atlantic Coast Conference era, the coliseum has grown in capacity from less than 7,000 (when it opened in 1956) to its current 9,191. The arena has hosted some of the South's best basketball, many of which came at the hands of Atlanta Sports Legends as Roger Kaiser and Rich Yunkus.

The facility retains its traditional name of Alexander Memorial Coliseum while recognizing the role of McDonald's, which contributed $5.5 million in a unique corporate partnership when the 1996 re-creation was done.

Alexander Memorial Coliseum at McDonald's Center also served as the boxing venue for the 1996 Centennial Olympic Games and was a temporary home for the NBA's Atlanta Hawks for the 1997-98 and 1998-99 seasons.

The coliseum was completed in September 1956 at a cost of approximately $1.6 million. It was built as a tribute to the late William Alexander, Tech's third athletics director and football coach from 1920-1944. Alexander wanted to provide Tech with a physical training center for all students, but he died in April 1950, before seeing the project completed.

Alexander Memorial Coliseum was dedicated on Nov. 30, 1956, when the Rambling Wreck lost to Duke, 71-61. The Jackets have posted three perfect seasons at home, including a 6-0 mark after the re-creation in 1995-96 as well as a 14-0 campaign in 1963-64 and a 9-0 slate in 1985-86.

The facility was given its nickname by former Tech radio announcer Brad Nessler during the 1983-84 season when the Jackets had five ACC home games decided in the final seconds, including a double-overtime win over Maryland; a triple-overtime victory over Virginia; and a last-second shot to beat Wake Forest.

ATLANTA-FULTON COUNTY STADIUM

Completed in just 50 weeks' time for $18 million, the facility opened in the spring of 1965 as Atlanta Stadium. It was intended as the home of the soon-to-be-relocating Braves, but court battles kept the team in Milwaukee as a lame duck for a year. So the new stadium had a lame duck of its own for that first season: the Atlanta Crackers of the International League, whose previous home had been Ponce de Leon Park.

In 1966, both Major League Baseball's transplanted Atlanta Braves and the NFL's expansion Atlanta Falcons moved in. The Falcons moved to the Georgia Dome in 1992, while the Braves had to wait until the Olympic Stadium from the 1996 Summer Olympics was renovated into Turner Field to move out at the beginning of the 1997 season.

Sitting 60,700 for football and 52,013 for baseball, the ballpark was relatively nondescript, one of the many saucer-shaped multipurpose facilities built during the 1960s. The field itself was long known for the poor quality – no one bothered to hire full-time groundskeepers until the early 1990s, instead relying on a city work crew. When then-new Braves General Manager John Schuerholz's came on board before the 1991 season, one of his first moves was to hire a quality grounds crew and improve the variety of concessions offered at the ballpark. As a result – along with the franchise's unprecedented winning streak – the stadium's reputation began to improve.

Relatively high elevation meant that the stadium was generally favorable to long-ball hitters, giving rise to the nickname, "the Launching Pad." That factor certainly helped boost Henry Aaron's home run output, and he reached the all-time record sooner here than he might have in Milwaukee. The stadium was refurbished for the 1996 season for Olympic baseball competition.

Atlanta-Fulton County Stadium was imploded on Aug. 2, 1997. A parking lot for Turner Field now stands on the site, with an outline of the old stadium, and a plaque marking the spot where Hank Aaron's historic 715th career home run landed on April 8, 1974, in what was formerly the Braves bullpen.

ATLANTA MUNICIPAL AUDITORIUM

In 1907, Atlanta had no one single facility large enough for indoor sporting events, civic occasions or where the militia could train. On Feb. 7, property was acquired at the intersection of Courtland and Gilmer streets to locate the newly formed Atlanta Auditorium-Armory Co.

Construction on the Municipal Auditorium began in 1907, and was completed in 1909. Newly elected President William Howard Taft spoke at the facility before the main arena had been completed; the room in which a banquet was served in his honor was dubbed Taft Hall, a moniker that continues in use today, as the structure now houses Georgia State University's Alumni Hall.

The auditorium's main arena could seat approximately 5,500 people. In the 1950s and '60s, in the facility's twilight years, professional wrestling matches were held every Friday night. Local promoter Paul Jones is said to have wrestled himself at the auditorium in the 1920s.

The most famous historical sports event in the auditorium's history came on Oct. 26, 1970, when Muhammad Ali returned to the ring after a three-year absence. The New York Boxing Commission and the World Boxing Association had stripped Ali of his title and barred him from fighting anywhere in the country because of his refusal to serve in the U.S. Army during the Vietnam War. State Sen. Leroy Johnson and Atlanta insurance executive Jesse Hill staged the bout at Atlanta City Auditorium, which saw Ali defeat Quarry in three rounds.

By the late 1960's, the auditorium had become a reliable venue for catching the latest touring rock acts, such as The Who, Pink Floyd, The Allman Brothers, Jimi Hendrix, The Grateful Dead, Frank Zappa, Little Feat, and Black Sabbath, among many others.

THE OMNI

It was like nothing Atlanta had ever seen when it opened in 1972. Its roof was likened to a waffle iron or an upside-down egg carton; and its exterior was designed to change color as the years went past. Twenty-five years after it was built, however, the facility was showing its age, and it was imploded to make room for the Philips Arena, which is built on the exact same architectural footprint as its predecessor.

The Omni served as the home of the NBA Atlanta Hawks; the NHL's Atlanta Flames between 1972-80; the home of the 1988 Democratic National Convention; and the International Hockey League's Atlanta Knights. The facility hosted countless shows, concerts, circuses, professional wrestling matches, indoor soccer, tennis, hockey, roller derby and even motocross races, not to mention basketball Final Fours for men and women, and the U.S. Figure Skating Championship in 1980. It also was the home of volleyball competition during the Atlanta Olympics.

The Omni's origins went back to 1968, when the Hawks moved from St. Louis to Atlanta with the promise of a new building. After playing on Georgia Tech's campus for four seasons, the Hawks finally moved to the $16 million coliseum, built at no cost to the taxpayers. Developer (and Atlanta Sports Legend) Tom Cousins, who owned the Hawks at the time, built the Omni atop a mass of railroad tracks in a desolate area of downtown, hoping the arena and an adjacent office and entertainment center would rejuvenate the area.

With a maximum seating capacity of 16,500, the Omni's first event came on Oct. 14, 1972, when the Flames tied the Buffalo Sabres 1-1. One day later, the Atlanta Hawks defeated the New York Knicks 109-101. Atlanta Sports Legend Lenny Wilkens became the winningest coach in NBA history in the Omni, surpassing Red Auerbach, when the Hawks beat the Washington Bullets 112-90, on Jan. 6, 1995.

The Omni helped Atlanta become one of the country's leading convention cities, as well as a center of professional sporting activities. It was imploded in 1997.

PONCE DE LEON BALLPARK

"Ol' Poncey" was one of the nation's finest minor league baseball facilities in the early to mid-twentieth century.

Shortly after the turn of the century, the original ballpark was built on property northeast of downtown owned by the Georgia Railway and Electric Company, directly across Ponce de Leon Avenue from an amusement park. A lake on the site was drained, filled in, and converted into a $60,000 ballpark made of wood. More than 8,000 fans welcomed the minor league Atlanta Crackers to their new home on May 23, 1907.

In 1923 the wooden ballpark burned down, and the Crackers finished out the season at Grant Field. Then a wealthy concessionaire named Rell Jackson Spiller spent $250,000 to build a concrete-and-steel masterpiece. When R. J. Spiller Field made its debut in time for the 1924 season, the Atlanta paper City Builder called it "the most magnificent park in the minor leagues."

The new facility drew lavish praise from baseball officials across the country. Chairs were fastened into the stadium's new concrete skeleton, furnishing seats that were far more comfortable than the wooden benches fans used to occupy. The grandstand's entire capacity was 9,800. The bleachers for the white fans, located in right field, accommodated 2,500, and the seats in left field, for black fans, held the same number. With standing room for more than 6,000, the stadium could hold 20,000.

The fence was 365 feet down the left field line, 321 to right, and 462 to dead center, where a giant magnolia stood.

Fans could entertain themselves by gambling, which Georgia law allowed when it wasn't conducted under a roof. The covered grandstands became home to the true Cracker faithful, and the outfield bleachers were host to the "fly-ball fans," who sat with the local oddsmakers. People would bet on anything, including on whether an outfielder would drop a routine fly ball. The Crackers called Ponce de Leon Ballpark home until their final season in 1965, when they moved into the newly built Atlanta Stadium. The ballpark was torn down in 1966, and the site has been home to numerous retail operations since then. The magnolia tree, however, still stands.

THE ATLANTA SPORTS HALL OF FAME

What was surprising to Larry Winter, founder and president of the Atlanta Sports Hall of Fame, was not so much that the city itself didn't have such an entity, but that virtually every other major Georgia municipality did.

"And, when I would travel around the country, I would visit other major cities' sports halls of fame, many of which are quite stunning," he says. "San Diego has the best city sports hall of fame that I've seen; housed in a big building, with an excellent cadre of educational programs and awards.

"Atlanta has such a great sports tradition," and yet the city didn't have its own method of recognizing the great sports heroes of its past and present.

With no million-dollar sponsors; with no official sanction from the city or any other local government; and with no display space or permanent office location, Winter set out to undertake the incredibly monumental task of creating an Atlanta Sports Hall of Fame.

"The biggest challenge in the beginning was convincing all of the people who I spoke with, and who thought it was a good idea, to roll up their sleeves and work," Winter recalls. "But not having any big-name sponsors or individuals on board has created an opportunity for people, including our retired volunteers - who have great skill sets and are still very active physically and emotionally - to get involved and excited over the effort, so they can say that they accomplished this themselves."

Winter built the Atlanta Sports Hall of Fame with the help of a dedicated group of volunteers and countless upon countless meetings with all of the city's major sports executives and officials, along with a solid business plan and budget. His dream became a reality in 2005, when the first class of Atlanta Sports Hall of Fame inductees were recognized: Hank Aaron, Bobby Cox, Bobby Dodd, Bobby Jones, Tommy Nobis, and Dominique Wilkins, all Atlanta Sports Legends.

"Even at the induction ceremony, some people were doubtful that individuals with the stature of Aaron and Nobis would attend," Winter says. "All of them attended (Cox, on the road with the Braves, accepted via a video link, and members of the Dodd and Jones families represented their famous relatives), and Hank said, with a big smile, that it was an honor to be in the inaugural class."

To date, the hall has inducted a total of four classes, many of whom are profiled within the pages of this book.

There is a three-tier process to select the inductees. The first step is done by the Selections and Nominations Committee, which is scheduled to occur each December. The second step is review by the Advisory Committee, which meets in January, while the final vote is performed by a group of Atlanta business and sports leaders called the "Honors Court" which, in the past, has been represented by such organizations as Georgia Tech; the Atlanta Falcons; the Atlanta Braves; Georgia State University; the Georgia State Golf Association; the *Atlanta Journal-Constitution*; the Atlanta Hawks; Comcast Sports Nite; 790 The Zone, Atlanta Sports Talk Radio; and *Points North* Magazine. The non-profit organization receives no state, county or city funds, but is operated entirely from donations by individuals and corporations.

Thanks to a lot of hard work and dedication from its founders, the Atlanta Sports Hall of Fame looks to grow in stature and recognition for years to come. Future display space is in the works, as are educational programs and other undertakings. "With all of the great individual organizations we have in Atlanta, such as track clubs and tip-off clubs, we hope to elevate their awareness as well," Winter says.

"We wanted to create a mechanism where people like Tommy Nobis are remembered and recognized. Aaron and Nobis – who were the Chipper Jones and Keith Brooking of their era, respectively - came to Atlanta at the same time, and even played golf together. Bobby Jones was born here, educated here, played here and died here. We should all be aware and proud of accomplishments and events such as these."

Larry Winter, founder and president, Atlanta Sports Hall of Fame

THE ATLANTA SPORTS COUNCIL

The Atlanta Sports Council promotes the value of sports growth in Atlanta and Georgia by acting as an authority on the economic impact, visibility and quality of life issues associated with sports. Its mission is to lead, organize and support sports development with the goal of building Atlanta's reputation as the Sports Capital of the World.

Since 1985, the Atlanta Sports Council has helped attract more than 60 sporting events to metro Atlanta including Super Bowls XXVIII (1994) and XXXIV (2000), the Centennial Olympic Games, the 1993 and 2003 Women's NCAA Final Four, 2002 and 2007 Men's Final Four, 1998, 2000 and 2002 TOUR Championship, 2000 Major League Baseball All-Star Game, 2001 PGA Championship, 2003 NBA All-Star Game and 2008 NHL All-Star Game.

Gary Stokan, president, Atlanta Sports Council and Chick-fil-A Bowl

The Atlanta Sports Council helps drive sports business in Atlanta and has become an expert in determining local and statewide economic impact from these events. In 1997, the Atlanta Sports Council commissioned a detailed study analyzing the business of sports in metro Atlanta . The Atlanta Sports Council Economic Impact Formula was developed in partnership with Atlanta-based McKinsey & Company and Dr. Bruce Seaman , Georgia State University economics professor and president of the Association for Cultural Economics. The formula provides an accurate approximation of the direct and induced economic impact generated by major sporting events.

The Atlanta Sports Council is responsible for helping drive more than $1 billion in economic impact to Atlanta from 1999-2006.

Gary Stokan currently serves as president of the Atlanta Sports Council is in his 10th year as president of the Atlanta Sports Council and the Chick-fil-A Bowl. Stokan is leading Atlanta 's efforts to brand the city as the Sports Capital of the World, drawing a range of world-caliber sporting events to metro Atlanta.

Named the 2002, 2004 and 2006 Sports Commission of the Year, the Atlanta Sports Council has successfully bid for Super Bowls, NCAA Men's and Women's Final Fours, PGA tournaments and the MLB, NBA and NHL All-Star Games. Stokan has also helped bring the ACC Men's Basketball Tournament, the USA Volleyball Junior Olympic Championships and the U.S. Women's Figure Skating Championships to the metro Atlanta.

Stokan, ranked the 16th most influential sports figure in Georgia, is a nationally recognized speaker and serves on the Board of the Children's Healthcare Sports, Atlanta Convention and Visitors Bureau and is president of the Atlanta Tipoff Club

Made in the USA
Charleston, SC
17 September 2010